Acknowledge

CW01079841

Quotes taken from the works of George Orwell;

"From The Road To Wigan Pier by George Orwell published by Martin Secker & Warburg Limited. Reproduced by permission of The Random House Group Ltd © 1959"

"From Narrative Essays by George Orwell published by Harvill Secker. Reproduced by permission of The Random House Group Ltd © 2009"

"From Critical Essays by George Orwell published by Harvill Secker. Reproduced by permission of The Random House Group Ltd © 2009"

The author would like to thank the following for help with the production of this book; The Orwell Institute, the staff of both Sheffield and Barnsley libraries and their respective local studies and reference sections, Penguin Random Publishers.

All Sheffield photographs courtesy of Sheffield City Archives and all Barnsley photographs courtesy of Barnsley Archives And Local Studies.

This book is dedicated to Gavin Talbot, born, lived and died in Barnsley. Odpočívej v pokoji

----

Front cover – an eastbound train emerges from the Woodhead Tunnel at Dunford Bridge, West Riding of Yorkshire in 1940

1

Introduction

I cannot recall exactly when I read George Orwell's The Road To Wigan Pier, his description of housing, health, environmental, industrial and working conditions in Wigan, Sheffield and Barnsley in 1936, for the first time but it would have been sometime in the 1970s or 1980s. I have to admit it didn't make much of an impression on me, not because it's not a great book but because I was born and brought up in one of these three places, Barnsley. A book about the surroundings you know better than anywhere else isn't going to hold the same interest for you that, for example, Homage to Catalonia, would. This, his next book after The Road To Wigan Pier, is a book I read about the same time and a book which, being about the foreign and exotic, even during a brutal civil war, would be of greater interest. The only thing I took from The Road To Wigan Pier at the time was that Barnsley had been just as grey and miserable in the 1930s as it was forty or so years later although you do get a bit of civic pride from your home town forming part of a work as lauded as Orwell's.

I read it again in about 2008 and for the second time I found it a disappointment. It was again just telling me things I had grown up in the middle of and to make things worse the language seemed so old-fashioned. With hindsight this was probably to do with the money quoted being in £sd and the fact that all the mines mentioned in it were by then closed. As time had moved on the details in the book had receded into history, becoming almost Dickensian. The background to the book rather than its content however did start to resonate with me and I started to look into the people Orwell had met and the places he had visited when he had been in Barnsley.

Two things stood out from researching Orwell's 1936 stay. First, the fact that Orwell lodged at 4, Agnes Terrace, a house that is still standing, unlike many others he visited at the time, and a house that is about 300 yards from where I was born and brought up, as well as being about 50 yards from where my first school was. Second was his visit to the Civic Hall, then called the Public Hall, on Eldon Street in the town centre where he saw the then British fascist leader Oswald Mosley speak and also saw the anti-fascist demonstrators, among them Tommy Degnan, whom Orwell subsequently met, discussed politics with and wrote about.

The following year both Orwell and Degnan were shot fighting Franco's forces in Spain albeit in different pro-Republican organisations. Both survived but left Spain shortly after.

After several drip-drip-drip years of discovering more and more anecdotes about Orwell's stay in Barnsley I read The Road To Wigan Pier for the third time in 2017 and finally the political relevance of the book hit home with me. So did the brilliance of some of the writing. I realised it wasn't the language that was old-fashioned. It was the fact that the book was now a historical tract rather than an out-of-date account of life as it was at the time that Orwell intended to write. Much of the housing and industry that he described in the book no longer exists. Many of the homes, factories and other buildings as well as all the mines are gone. But it brings back to life the working class life of Wigan, Sheffield and Barnsley in 1936. And having read in the intervening years Orwell's contemporaneous diaries and notes and narratives about his stay that he used a background material when subsequently writing the book, it was obvious that he had left far more of his stay in Barnsley out of the book than he had included. If The Road To Wigan Pier deserves detailed analysis and repeated attention so does the background research that Orwell undertook that its writing was based on.

Likewise, he also left much of the detail of his stay in Sheffield out of the book, and much of the housing and industry of the city that existed in 1936 has also gone. In chapter 4 of the book he mentioned a visit to Thomas Street in Sheffield. I had to look up in the A-Z where Thomas Street is. It is actually about 300 yards from where I live now and is a street so nondescript that I had walked down it hundreds of times without knowing what it was called, never mind that it was mentioned in a book as famous as Orwell's. It is today just nothing more than a cut-through to the shops or wherever and is also about just a third of the length it was in 1936 with barely any building surviving from that time. Make-shift car parks, bland post-war buildings and wasteland make up a lot of what is left of it. There aren't even any trees for the council to cut down, or at least perhaps there aren't anymore. All the houses are gone. The house that Orwell visited there has been replaced with a tile warehouse which is itself due to be replaced in the coming years by a complex of student accommodation, because Sheffield is short of that sort of thing.

The Britain that Orwell was writing about in 1936 was already in flux, especially in housing, one of the main themes of the book. Industrial transformation came decades later. He acknowledged as such when he wrote about the slums that were then being cleared and the new estates that were being built. In fact, Sheffield had cleared some of its first slums over 30 years earlier and had already built its first council housing, initially as flats and later as housing estates. In the nearly twenty years from the end of the First World War in 1918 to 1936, Liberal, Labour, Conservative and National governments had passed housing laws to rid the country of the slums that Orwell describes in the book and to build new, more habitable homes.

The catalyst to this had been the horrific death toll of the First World War and the subsequent massive extending of the franchise. Orwell didn't mention the political and social background of these changes in detail, mainly just the daily grind of life, as it was his agenda following a suggestion from his publisher, Victor Gollancz, to detail the deprivation of life in the industrial north. And when he did mention the new estates he was not entirely welcoming of the idea.

So here we have this posh old Etonian over eighty years ago, having been lodged in one house 300 yards from where I was later born and writing about another house that had been 300 yards from where I now live nearly sixty years later. It's as if the bloke was stalking me over twenty years before I was born. Intrigued I decided to look into all the other aspects of his stay in Sheffield and Barnsley in as much detail as I could - where else he had stayed and visited, who else he had met and what else he had done during his stay here. And as the details emerged so did the bigger historical context - how the Britain that Orwell was then writing about was changing even at the time, how it had become what it already was by 1936 and how it would change again during the rest of his life and after his death. Those missing two thirds of Thomas Street must have gone somewhere and for a reason.

Given that, as much as Orwell put in the book, he left out so much of the background experiences he had while doing his research in Lancashire and Yorkshire, the aim of this book is to explore and explain the Barnsley and Sheffield of March 1936 that Orwell experienced while researching The Road To Wigan Pier but didn't mention in the book, and also explain some of what he did write about. The starting point, other than The Road To Wigan Pier itself, are the diaries and notes and narratives that Orwell wrote at the time and which have been published separately. Other sources include library collections, websites, radio and television programs, films, old photos and maps, word of mouth and visiting the actual places that Orwell visited, sometimes along Thomas Street on the way to the shops. This book is essentially a local history project with a national figure at its centre. Orwell wrote about Sheffield and Barnsley and by doing so created a story that has been told in parts in many different articles, books and films which need to be brought together in detail with other information that has not yet been aired or at least not in the context of The Road To Wigan Pier, in order to describe the fuller picture of Orwell's stay in one Yorkshire town and one Yorkshire city. Lancashire might get all the publicity but we were there too.

Orwell though wasn't the first person to cross the Pennines to look at industrial and living conditions. Friedrich Engels' The Condition of the Working Class in England was a similar study from nearly hundred years earlier, 1844, which detailed the working and living conditions of people over a wider area of England including, as Engels put it, Scotland, Wales and Ireland! The date coincided with an era of a massive expansion of Sheffield's steel industry.

It's quite possible that Orwell had read this work. In 1938 his wife Sonia wrote that they had called their new dog Marx, after Karl Marx, as a reminder that they had never read his works. However, Orwell was said years later by Richard Rees, editor of Adelphi magazine for which Orwell wrote, to have in fact already been quite knowledgeable in 1936 about the works of Engels' close colleague Karl Marx. If so then he could easily have read Engels as well. He certainly seemed to have known enough Marxists, as he explains in the second part of the book, which he ends with a pun on the most famous line of the most famous book by Marx and Engels. And in 1937 he was in Spain as a member of the *Partido Obrero de Unificación Marxista.*

There are some strikingly similar observations between Engels' and Orwell's books including about the physical size of the miners, their working conditions and wages, poor general living conditions including the common privy middens (shared outside toilets), and poor public health. A comparison between the two works shows that in some areas

5

little had changed in the almost hundred years between Engels' and Orwell's studies.

The title of this book, The Train From Wigan Pier, is not intended solely to reflect Orwell's preferred means of transport for crossing from Lancashire to Yorkshire via Derbyshire, but also the importance of the railway in the urban industrial landscape at the time, especially of Sheffield. For example, Orwell lodged in Parkwood Springs, an area of Sheffield that was built for rail workers in the 19th century and whose housing had been entirely destroyed by the late 1970s, partly by German bombs and partly by bulldozers following the orders of government housing legislation. Parkwood Springs was an area which had only two entry and exit points, one a road under a railway line and the other a pedestrian bridge over the same line. Both still exist today but now lead mainly to and from what is largely a wasteland.

It was railway that greatly facilitated the industrialisation of Britain and it was industrial Britain that Orwell wrote about in The Road To Wigan Pier. It was also a railway line, the Woodhead line, that on the eastern side of the Pennines ran parallel with the river Don upon which a lot of Sheffield steel was manufactured. And it was the Woodhead line that served some of the coalfields of Barnsley and of Sheffield. Sheffield's coal industry has been greatly overlooked, not just by Orwell, due to Sheffield steel being so dominant a part of the city's industrial history. Orwell didn't mention it at all. Much of that industrial Britain of 1936, including the coalfields, a lot of the steel industry and even most of the train line that passed by where Orwell stayed in Sheffield, as well as the house itself, indeed the entire housing area, no longer exist.

When I write of The Road To Wigan Pier I am writing mainly of the first half of the book, the first seven chapters which deal with Orwell's experiences in Wigan, Sheffield and Barnsley. These focus on the effects of heavy industry on people's working and living conditions, environment, health and people in the places he visited. The second half I largely ignore except where it complements the first half. Otherwise it has little direct relationship to Orwell's stay in Lancashire and Yorkshire in February and March 1936, being largely an essay on his own preferred political solutions to the problems he highlighted in the first part. As far as I can tell the only person he names in part 2 who ever went down a pit was DH Lawrence, said by Orwell's biographer Bernard Crick to have gone down Wentworth Silkstone pit in Barnsley, which may have influenced Orwell's decision to go down it too. He refers to many miners, as well as to others he met in February and March 1936, in part two, especially Tommy Degnan, but doesn't name them.

That isn't to say that part two is less important a piece of Orwell's writing, but that there is no smoke or sulphur in it and this being a book about South Yorkshire it must be about smoke, Sulphur, muck and grass, or what little of the last Orwell saw under the snow on the moors from his train window as he approached Sheffield, even though the politics rather than the industry may have been more important to him. Ten years after writing The Road To Wigan Pier, Orwell explained in Why I Write; *"The Spanish war and other events in 1936-37 turned the scale and thereafter I knew where I stood"*, meaning his political views had become clear due to what he witnessed in Lancashire, Yorkshire, Aragon and Catalonia. The effects of the industrialism in Yorkshire are part of what shaped Orwell's clearer political outlook and are what I will concentrate on here. Orwell was essentially a political writer and in his own words his experiences in 1936 and 1937 in Lancashire, Yorkshire and Spain shaped his politics more than any other time and places.

Orwell wrote one story of industrialism in the north of England and this is the story of Orwell in Barnsley and Sheffield writing that story. I leave Wigan out of the picture as it has already had enough publicity and I have no personal experience of living there. Orwell's book bears its name and Lancashire already gets all the publicity, good or bad. There are plaques and buildings in Wigan commemorating his stay there whereas Barnsley and Sheffield have no such official commemoration. In May 2018 when covering the unveiling of a plaque to Orwell in Wigan the Granada Television reporter claimed that not only was Orwell's book only about the North West but that Orwell actually wrote it in Wigan. Wigan Pier is even marked on atlases and there is also a motorway sign on the M61 directing people to the area of the town on the Leeds-Liverpool Canal where a century ago coal from mines on the Winstanley Estate a couple of miles west was transported by tram and loaded onto barges from a jetty with the ironic nickname that Orwell used for the title of his book.

Lancashire also has the deserved honour and fame for having given us L S Lowry whose paintings of industrial northern England have brought its environment, industry and people to a far wider audience than Orwell has, even if Lowry's romantic depictions of urban industrialism, the spark for which was triggered by Lancashire's canals, mills, urban wastelands, railways and pits, lacked the horror of daily life that Orwell set out to expose. Compare Lowry's 1955 painting *Industrial Landscape* to Orwell's hellish description of Sheffield's Attercliffe in chapter 7. Both are scenes of chimneys, railways, pollution, gasworks, slum housing and mills but Orwell's isn't the kind of scene you'd want to hang on your living room wall.

Yorkshire, for once in its life, has not blown its own trumpet loudly enough. For example, while writing this book I was on holiday in Tarragona, a Catalan town where Orwell spent time in hospital in 1937 after being shot. In the library there I was reading a Spanish translation of his essays which gave background information on his life including the assertion that in 1936, while preparing to write The Road To Wigan Pier, Orwell spent time researching working class life in the Lancashire towns of Wigan, Sheffield and Barnsley. The frustration was relieved only by my discovering that the library I was in was situated on the corner of the Carrer del Gasometre. The irony will become clear if you turn the page and read on.

Sheffield

On Monday 2nd March 1936 George Orwell left Wigan and travelled by train to Sheffield via Manchester. Then aged thirty two he was already a published writer and journalist and had just spent a month in Lancashire - Manchester, Wigan and Liverpool - researching material for what would be his second book of non-fiction and his fifth in all, The Road To Wigan Pier. Altogether he published nine books in his lifetime. His first, a book of non-fiction, Down And Out in Paris And London, had been published just three years earlier in 1933 and been followed by two novels, Burmese Days the following year and A Clergyman's Daughter in 1935. His third novel, Keep the Aspidistra Flying, had already been completed and would be published the following month, April 1936. All but Burmese Days were published by Victor Gollancz Ltd, a socialist publisher, who had suggested to him that he visit northern England to write a study of unemployment and poverty there. It was this suggestion that had brought him to Lancashire and Yorkshire and which would produce The Road To Wigan Pier.

Orwell's research in Lancashire had been concentrated in the town whose name the new book would bear, Wigan, and was particularly centred on the working conditions of the miners, the appalling housing conditions of the old slums, the environmental effects of industrialisation and the poverty of unemployment. Orwell would continue with these themes over the Pennines in Sheffield and Barnsley. He seems to have had little previous personal experience of northern England other than to have visited his sister who lived in Leeds with her husband.

Wigan had been suggested to him for its mines by a working-class writer and activist in the National Unemployed Workers Movement (NUWM) in Rochdale, Jack Hilton, whose book Caliban Shrieks Orwell had reviewed positively in 1935 in Adelphi, a literary magazine Orwell had contributed to regularly since 1931. Frank Meade of the magazine's Manchester office, with whom Orwell initially lodged, referred him to Jerry Kennan in Wigan who in turn referred him to Paddy Grady, a NUWM activist in Wigan, when Orwell got there. Grady subsequently recommended that Orwell meet Tommy Degnan in Barnsley. Kennan arranged Orwell's first visit down a pit and accompanied him. Orwell's reference points were therefore initially literary, both working- and middle-class and not solely industrial and politically-organised working class even though the object of his research would be the latter. Orwell was essentially a literary figure researching a people, the local industry and an environment of which he had never had any direct personal experience before. This meant that he began with literary contacts which led him to industrial contacts who would take him round the local industry. In Sheffield that meant he was researching the steel industry.

It's not known by which route he travelled from Lancashire to Yorkshire, whether he changed trains in Manchester or travelled direct. In 1936 it was possible to travel from Manchester to Sheffield by three routes - the Caldervale route via Bradford, Halifax and Huddersfield, the Hope Valley line through the Derbyshire Peak District and the Woodhead line between the two. If he had travelled by either of the last two routes, Woodhead or Hope valley, he would have travelled at least three miles underground in one of the two Victorian rail tunnels - Woodhead and Totley - that linked Derbyshire and Yorkshire, taking him back below the Earth's surface though hardly close to the harsh experience he had just spent underground in a Lancashire pit or close to getting him ready for more to come in Yorkshire.

If he caught a direct train from Wigan to Sheffield, originating in Liverpool, he is most likely to have travelled via the Woodhead line. This line opened in the mid-19th century principally as an industrial line to transport coal from south Yorkshire to Cheshire and Lancashire, and was the first railway line to open between the then two great industrialising cities of Sheffield and Manchester. It would also have been the most appropriate line for him to have travelled by. The Woodhead line was engineered by Joseph Locke who was born in Attercliffe, Sheffield and grew up in Barnsley where the main park is named after him. His engineering feats though are to be seen more in Sheffield where the Wardsend viaduct, built of five railway arches, carried the Woodhead line over Herries Road in Hillsborough, coincidentally just a mile or so from where Orwell would stay for his three-day visit. Barnsley however has the magnificently-named Rumtickle viaduct which took the line over a valley in Thurgoland several miles north. The Woodhead line would have taken him straight into the centre of Sheffield's heavy industry whose "*interminable vista of factory chimneys*" as Orwell described it was round the line's passenger terminus, Victoria Station, an area Orwell would visit and write about in The Road To Wigan Pier.

The Woodhead line was built by the Sheffield, Ashton-under-Lyne and Manchester Railway which subsequently became the Manchester, Sheffield and Lincolnshire Railway in 1847, two years after the line had opened. This name can still be seen on the Wicker arches just north of the city centre which carried the line from its original terminus at Bridgehouses to its approach to Sheffield Victoria Station, its now-demolished eastern passenger terminus, built to extend the line to industry further east. The Wicker arches mark the end of the city centre and the start of industrial east Sheffield.

From Manchester at its western end the Woodhead line ran to Glossop and Hadfield in Derbyshire and from there into the Woodhead tunnel. On the east side of the Pennines it emerged from the tunnel at Dunford Bridge, a small hamlet west of Barnsley. From there it rolled east and then south towards Sheffield following the River Don down through Penistone, Deepcar, Oughtibridge, Hillsborough, Neepsend, Kelham Island and Bridgehouses to Victoria Station just east of the Wicker arches, its entrance to the station. The line ended a couple of miles further east at Rotherwood sidings, then a mining area.

An extension of the line south east from Penistone to Wath, the Worsbrough branch, served the collieries of Barnsley and was used to ferry coal from there over the Pennines. The main line, especially from Hillsborough to Victoria Station, ran down past the heavy industry, particularly steel-making, of Sheffield. After Victoria Station, the track served the collieries of east and south east Sheffield and Rotherham as well as onward passenger services to Nottinghamshire and Lincolnshire. Close to Victoria Station, opposite Wicker arches, was Wicker Station, Sheffield's first.

By the mid-19th century when the Sheffield to Rotherham and Woodhead lines opened, boosted by the opening of the Sheffield & Tinsley Canal which was built to transport goods and raw materials as parts of the Don weren't navigable, Sheffield was already producing half of Europe's steel and ninety percent of Britain's. Steel was replacing cutlery as Sheffield's main industry and over the next forty years its

11

output would grow tenfold, from 10,000 tons in 1835 to 100,000 tons in 1873.

Sheffield had been producing cutlery for centuries due to the constant flow of water in its rivers, the Don, Sheaf, Loxley, Rivelin and Porter, which initially could power water wheels and later provided steam power, and could be used for the bellows, hammers and grinding wheels of the mills and factories. It was the Sheaf that gave the city its name as well as some of its industry. The nearby availability of coal from Barnsley, east and south east Sheffield, Rotherham and the north Midlands provided carbon for the steel-making process.

The growth had been stimulated by the opening of Sheffield's first railway line, from Wicker Station to Rotherham and by the invention of the Bessemer process by Henry Bessemer which speeded up the process of steel manufacturing and thereby made mass production of steel possible. In so doing he turned Sheffield into an important industrial city. The Don and Sheaf, as the widest and most powerful rivers, were the most useful for cooling processes and for having industrial effluence discharged into them. Consequently, many of the new steel works that opened following this development were based in that area, near Wicker Station and Victoria Station, on both sides of the Sheffield to Rotherham line and on both sides of the nearby Don, where the Sheaf flowed into it near the former site of Sheffield Castle. The massive growth of the steel industry in the mid- to late-nineteenth century was centered on Savile Street, Effingham Street, Furnival Road, Effingham Road, Foley Street, Sussex Street, Sussex Road and Carlisle Street. Demand for steel was driven by the growth of the railways and by the expansion of the British Empire. Major steel works established in the area were the Sheaf Works, Atlas Works, Cyclops Works, Aetna Works and Norfolk Works. The industrialist names of Cammell, Firth, Brown and Jessop drove the expansion.

At the end of chapter I of The Road To Wigan Pier Orwell describes leaving the scarred man-made industrial urban landscape of Wigan by train for the countryside, largely unspoilt by man, before approaching Sheffield (Manchester isn't mentioned). He wrote; "*For quite a long time, perhaps another twenty minutes, the train was rolling through open country before the villa-civilization began to close in upon us again, and then the outer slums, and then the slag-heaps, belching chimneys, blast-furnaces, canals, and gasometers of another industrial town."*

Sheffield. This is Sheffield.

Orwell lodged at 154 Wallace Road in Parkwood Springs, next to the Woodhead line and close to the River Don. The area of Parkwood Springs was a small community of half a dozen or so streets built by railway companies just east of Neepsend Station and a couple of miles north of Sheffield city centre. It had just two entrances to it, and still has, although all the housing has now been demolished. A road under the railway bridge at the south end from Bardwell Road to Douglas Road is still there as is the pedestrian railway bridge, now a different one to the one during Orwell's visit, over the line where Neepsend Station used to be. The station closed in 1940 due to low public use.

The residents of 154 Wallace Road were Kathleen (Kate) and Gilbert Searle as well as a lodger, William Brown, a writer for The Adelphi. The residence was recommended to Orwell for the left-wing politics of the hosts. Kate Searle was in the Labour Party. Brown, who would be Orwell's guide round Sheffield for the next couple of days, was a communist and Orwell's point of contact. For two days Brown, despite being disabled, dragged Orwell round the slums and heavy industry of Sheffield leaving the following impression on the writer that he noted in chapter VII of The Road To Wigan Pier;

"Sheffield, I suppose, could justly claim to be called the ugliest town in the Old World: its inhabitants, who want it to be pre-eminent in everything, very likely do make that claim for it. It has a population of half a million and it contains fewer decent buildings than the average East Anglian village of five hundred. And the stench! If at rare moments you stop smelling sulphur it is because you have begun smelling gas. Even the shallow river that runs through the town is usually bright yellow with some chemical or other. Once I halted in the street and counted the factory chimneys I could see; there were thirty-three of them, but there would have been far more if the air had not been obscured by smoke. One scene especially lingers in my mind. A frightful patch of waste ground (somehow, up there, a patch of waste ground attains a squalor that would be impossible even in London) trampled bare of grass and littered with newspapers and old saucepans. To the

right an isolated row of gaunt four-roomed houses, dark red, blackened by smoke. To the left an interminable vista of factory chimneys, chimney beyond chimney, fading away into a dim blackish haze. Behind me a railway embankment made of the slag from furnaces. In front, across the patch of waste ground, a cubical building of red and yellow brick, with the sign 'Thomas Grocock, Haulage Contractor'".

Orwell had written a similar passage in his diary entry for 5th March after he had already left Sheffield for Leeds. The main difference is that in his diary entry he got the name of the Haulage Contractor right. It was John, not Thomas, Grocock. Orwell presumably changed the name to hide the location. This was the junction of Lumley Street and Worthing Road in Attercliffe, about a mile east of Victoria Station. What was then the wasteland now has a steel company and hydraulics factory on it so that the view Orwell had in 1936 is no longer possible.

The "*interminable vista of factory chimneys*" to Orwell's left is gone too and was located in the area of steelworks just north of Victoria Station and the Wicker arches to Carlisle Street and across Savile Street to Effingham Road on either side of the river Don and Wicker Station. In other words, it was the area described above, the heart of Sheffield's steel-making industry. Today the only industrial chimney he would be able to see looking from Worthing Road in the direction he did in 1936 is that of the Bernard Road Waste Incinerator. The shallow river yellow with chemicals was the Don, the river that emerged at Dunford Bridge with the Woodhead line and ran down to Sheffield alongside it. As the widest river in Sheffield it was most useful as a means of flushing away industrial discharge, hence the yellow colour. Orwell had adopted his pen name from the Suffolk river due to his fondness for it. He obviously felt less fond of the Don.

The railway banking behind him was that of the Woodhead line just before Woodburn Junction although Orwell wouldn't have been able to see the tracks. Today all the old industrial tracks have been lifted but there is one track in each direction for the Sheffield to Lincoln line a mile or two east of Sheffield Midland Station before Darnall. A new wasteland has developed however at the top of the same railway embankment above the old one where the old industrial rail tracks were lifted and the land left unused. It is visible next to the track on the left on a Sheffield to Lincoln train or from a tram near Nunnery Square station.

Gone too are the gaunt four-roomed houses which would have been on Woodbourn Road, Woodbourn Hill and Ripon Street. The only surviving home there is the Woodbourne Hotel on the corner of Worthing Road and Lovetot Road. This area is otherwise now an industrial estate. Still there however is the cubical building of red and yellow brick (calling the brick yellow today is being generous) albeit no longer with the Grocock haulage sign. Today it is a recycling centre although it was lucky to survive a large fire in 2013 which spread from another building nearby on Worthing Road and damaged other neighbouring properties. The Sheffield & Tinsley Canal runs behind it, hidden from view. The canal basin was a mile west, back towards Victoria Station, where coal from nearby collieries was loaded onto barges. If Sheffield had its equivalent of Wigan Pier this is where it would have been. Orwell doesn't appear to have gone looking for it as he had the Wigan one.

The image Orwell painted may have been bleak but it could have been worse if he'd also been able to see over the railway line behind him. Directly behind him was the Sheffield abattoir and over his right shoulder was Nunnery Colliery. If he'd had those in his sights as well he could have mixed blood and coal into the vista of factory chimneys and written something that made Dante's inferno look like a tourist guide to the French Riviera.

Orwell hadn't been the first person to count chimneys in Sheffield however. In 1891, over forty years earlier, Henry Littlejohn was appointed Sheffield's Medical Officer of Health, a post he held for six years. After a lot of counting he published a report in 1897 in which he listed over 600 tall chimneys that poured out the smoke of over 800 steam boiler furnaces, another 138 chimneys from which the smoke of 266 steam boiler furnaces and 383 metallurgical furnaces was discharged, and nearly another thousand chimneys from which the smoke of metallurgical chimneys belched. Even then other industrial chimneys and all domestic chimneys weren't included in Littlejohn's much more interminable vista. Orwell's 1936 vista was little more than a snapshot.

Orwell's assertion that Sheffield contains "*fewer decent buildings than the average East Anglian village of five hundred*" is surprising given that on the evening of Tuesday 3rd March he went to the Victoria Hall

15

Methodist Church on Norfolk Street in the city centre. The building is now grade II listed. He also in his diary wrote that he went to Sheffield Town Hall and presumably passed The Cathedral Church of St Marie between the two. I don't know East Anglia's villages very well but I doubt many have buildings to rival these and others in Sheffield. Admittedly he says the air was obscured by smoke but he noticed the chimneys clearly enough to count them.

What he was more than likely distracted by was the slum housing he was to see after visiting church. Tuesday at the Victoria Hall Methodist Church was Men's Own night where the Rev. A C Austin MA gave a lecture on "Clean And Dirty Water" after a reading from Mark 11 verses 1-11. Orwell was at the event with William Brown and a friend of Brown's, John Binns. Unable to bear the excitement, despite the subject's clear relevance to the pollution of the Don as Orwell had witnessed earlier that day, they left early to go to Binns' home located about a mile west in what Orwell described in his diary as "t*he central, slummy part of the town"*. Welcome to Broomhall.

John and Mabel Binns lived with their four children at 13/2 Thomas Street in Broomhall on the western edge of the city centre quite close to the main shopping area of The Moor. The 13 stood for court 13 and 2 was the house number. There were only two inhabited houses in court 13, although others had over ten, backing on to houses that fronted Thomas Street itself. The Binns' home, like much of Broomhall's housing was back-to-back and backed on to the row of front houses of Thomas Street in the vicinity of number 109 almost opposite to and just north of the junction with Hodgson Street.

The house is mentioned in chapter IV of the book where Orwell describes the housing as follows; "'*Back to back' houses are two houses built in one, each side of the house being somebody's front door, so that if you walk down a row of what is apparently twelve houses you are in reality seeing not twelve houses but twenty-four. The front houses give on the street and the back ones on the yard, and there is only one way out of each house. The effect of this is obvious. The lavatories are in the yard at the back, so that if you live on the side facing the street, to get to the lavatory or the dust-bin you have to go out of the front door and walk round the end of the block--a distance that may be as much as two hundred yards; if you live at the back, on the other hand, your outlook is on to a row of lavatories....For it is to be noted that the majority of these houses are old, fifty or sixty years old at least, and great numbers of them are by any ordinary standard not fit for human habitation.... Towns like Leeds and Sheffield have scores of thousands of 'back to back' houses which are all of a condemned type but will remain standing for decades. "*

Orwell's estimate of the number of back-to-backs in Sheffield was a little high even if he was to be proved right about the number of years some of them would last. Some weren't cleared until the 1960s even though they were empty and derelict for years. Between the start and end of the nineteenth century Sheffield's population boomed, along with its industry, from under a hundred thousand to nearly half a million with most of the growth happening in the second half of the century with the boom of the steel industry. In 1864 there were 38,000 back-to-back houses in Sheffield when a bye-law prohibiting the building of any more was passed. They were built by private landlords as cheaply as possible and badly maintained if maintained at all down the years.

There was little government intervention to improve them. The Housing of the Working Classes Act 1885 was merely a health act that only allowed councils to condemn slum housing. Tenants must have been gratefully ecstatic. The Housing of the Working Classes Act 1890 allowed only the London County Council to compulsory buy land and build tenement and estate housing. In 1900 however, these powers were extended to other urban councils by the Housing of the Working Classes Act 1900. Sheffield subsequently cleared slums in the Crofts behind the cathedral and built its first council housing at Townhead nearby shortly after.

After a slow start the First World War was the catalyst for much greater changes in the nation's housing. In 1917 the Tudor Walters Committee Report recommended housing reforms in the light of soldier recruits being unfit for battle due to bad living conditions. In chapter VI of The Road To Wigan Pier Orwell wrote of the 1936 population *"The physical average in the industrial towns is terribly low, lower even than in London. In Sheffield you have the feeling of walking among a population of troglodytes"* although he put this down to bad diet, unemployment and industrialism in general.

17

At the 1918 general election Lloyd George campaigned on the slogan of a land fit for heroes with promises of improved conditions in health, education and housing. The Housing, Town Planning, &c. Act 1919 was passed under the stewardship of Christopher Addison, then a Liberal MP in the new government and later a Labour MP. The act provided finance to councils with the aim of building half a million new homes although fewer than half that number were built under it.

Under the next Conservative government, The Housing, &c. Act 1923 withdrew housing subsidies to councils in favour of private builders but this was in turn reversed by the Housing (Financial Provisions) Act 1924 passed by the first Labour government under the tutelage of John Wheatley, an Irish-Scots ex-miner. However, although over half a million new homes were consequently built the slums were not being cleared in sufficient numbers. The Housing Act 1930 of the second Labour government and led by Arthur Greenwood, a Yorkshireman representing a Lancashire seat and later Wakefield, encouraged slum clearance. Five years later the Housing Act 1935 under the National Government required every council to draw up a program of house building and demolition in order to get rid of all slums from their area. It also introduced a national standard to determine overcrowding. It was the background to and results of these acts of legislation that Orwell was witnessing in Wigan, Liverpool, Sheffield, Leeds and Barnsley in 1936.

The 1920s didn't just see the first Labour government but also the first Labour council in a British city, Sheffield in 1926. Like the housing legislation above, the catalyst for this came from the reaction to the slaughter of the First World War and the Representation of the People Act 1918 which tripled the number of eligible voters to 22 million by abolishing almost all property requirements for men over 21 and gave women over 30 the vote for the first time, subject to some property requirements.

Orwell writes in The Road To Wigan Pier somewhat critically of the new homes that Sheffield City Council had built and was building in the 1920s and 1930s as a result of the above legislation, especially about their location in the suburbs further from workplaces than the slums were, and the fact that they were (understandably) more expensive, which all sounded a bit rich coming from someone whose last two home addresses in London had been in Kentish Town and Hampstead. Further, at the start of chapter IV he writes that the slum houses he condemns *"are distributed in incredibly filthy slums round belching foundries and stinking canals and slag-heaps that deluge them with sulphorous smoke"* which begs the question as to where Orwell thought the new homes should be if they shouldn't be built in the suburbs or in the inner-city. Still, it was the conditions of the slums that had been targeted by government legislation for clearance and replacement that Orwell concentrated on.

The Binns' home at 13/2 Thomas Street was a case in point and he highlighted it in chapter IV of the book, the only Sheffield home he mentions there. Court 13 was off the north side of Court 15 which ran off the east side of Thomas Street just north of and opposite the junction with Hodgson Street. At the eastern end of Court 15 was the back of the Peacock Inn at 198-200 Fitzwilliam Street just up from the junction with Button Row, now Charter Row. Orwell mentions of the occupants; *"Six in family, parents and four children. Husband (on P.A.C.) is tuberculous."* P.A.C were Public Assistance Committees, means-tested welfare benefits. Illnesses such as TB were common due to living conditions although at least cholera had been eradicated by then. In the 19th century Sheffield, like other British cities, had suffered a number of cholera outbreaks exacerbated by open sewers and the common shared outside toilets, privy middens. Sheffield has a Cholera Monument built about half a mile east of Thomas Street to commemorate the 402 local victims of the 1832 outbreak.

Post-war rebuilding has changed the lay-out of the area. Only the middle part of Thomas Street is still a street. The bottom part, south of Moore Street has disappeared under post-war buildings at Moorfoot. The top part, north of Egerton Street, became a new council estate of concrete blocks of 650 flats in the 1960s which was subsequently knocked down to make way for another one of flats and houses in the 1990s. This still stands. At the north end of this and where the north end of Thomas Street used to meet Broomhall Street and Cavendish Street, Springfield School still stands. Just about everything else however has gone.

13/2 Thomas Street itself was possibly destroyed by German bombing during World War II although it is just as likely to have been abandoned and left empty. The Binns lived there until the start of the war but by the end had moved. There are huge gaps in the 1945 electoral register for the

19

east side of Thomas Street. No one was registered between numbers 29 and 89 and from there no one until number 125 which was the Sportsman pub just below where the Binns had lived. That isn't to say all the back-to-back homes there had been demolished. Many in Broomhall did stay standing empty and derelict for decades after. However German bombing completely destroyed the Moor shopping area, just south of Thomas Street and some homes nearby must have been hit. Just a couple of hundred yards north bombs fell on parts of Fitzwilliam Street, Broomhall Street and Devonshire Street killing people and destroying homes. After the rebuilding of the area, a tiles warehouse now stands where 13/2 Thomas Street used to stand although there are plans to build a new residential complex of flats on the site.

In 1936 Broomhall was a largely residential area of streets and lanes built in a grid system. There were businesses but like the houses in the area few of them survive. One that does is the Eye Witness Works on Milton Street and which may be the reference point for the following quote from Orwell's diary entry for March 4th; "*In the central slummy part of the town are the small workshops of the 'little bosses', i.e. smaller employers who are making chiefly cutlery. I don't think I ever in my life saw so many broken windows. Some of these workshops have hardly a pane of glass in their windows and you would not believe they were inhabitable if you did not see the employees, mostly girls, at work inside*". Cutlery-making still takes place at the Beehive Works on Milton Street next door.

Eye Witness Works is about 30 yards north of where the Binns' former home was and along with St Silas School on Hodgson Street, now converted to flats, is the only building surviving in the immediate vicinity of 13/2 Thomas Street from when Orwell visited it. Its design is a magnificent example of Sheffield's Victorian industrial heritage but the building is now neglected and in need of restoration. About 70 yards in length it backs on to one of the few surviving partly-cobbled lanes (where the tarmac has worn away), Egerton Lane, and although parts of it at the back have been demolished enough of it survives to be of some potential use. Plans have been announced to convert it to flats. Compare its present state to what has been done to similar industrial buildings at Elsecar Heritage Centre in Barnsley, Kelham Island, Aizlewood Mill in Nursery Street alongside the Don at Bridgehouses or the canal basin at

Victoria Quay in Sheffield, and it could be similarly magnificent if the investment works. And it's got a chimney.

After the war-time bombing the area around the Moor was redeveloped in the classic post-war Sheffield brutalist style. The Moor, when rebuilt, did not look much different to post-war Dresden as the architects sought to turn parts of Sheffield into the Florence of concrete, straight lines of large ugly grey boxes, the worst of all being the Moore Street electricity substation just 100 yards west of where 13/2 Thomas Street stood. Over time Broomhall east and west of Fitzwilliam Street changed. Much more has changed east, closer to the city centre, as businesses moved in. Thousands of students live there today and there is other city centre accommodation.

When I grew up in the 1960s and 1970s very few people lived in town and city centres. They weren't considered to be places anyone should live. When the old slum housing of Broomhall was either cleared or left derelict, little new inner-city housing was built there to replace it. The building of new housing was concentrated in the suburbs. In the last couple of decades however there has been much new development, especially of flats in the city centre. As a result of this and of the initial post-war redevelopment, the street plan of Broomhall, especially east of Fitzwilliam Street has been transformed.

The old grid system of streets and lanes has largely gone especially down towards Charter Row, formerly Button Row. Both that and the Moor are entirely post-war. The north end though by Division Street, Devonshire Street and West Street has kept a lot of its old buildings. Devonshire Green, part of the Devonshire Quarter which now disassociates itself from the Broomhall it was once part of, is a green space where streets of old back-to-back houses once stood and were torn down or bombed. Chester Street, like other streets and lanes which ran across it, has disappeared completely. Fitzwilliam Street has just a few pre-war buildings left including the Washington pub and a few shops at the north end by the junction with West Street and Glossop Road.

The changes on the west side of Fitzwilliam Street before the ring road have been a little less dramatic in the south end near where 13/2 Thomas Street stood, west to the ring road. Off Thomas Street the old housing has largely gone although a couple of houses on Milton Street survive and old industrial buildings other than Eye Witness Works are still there. Some later industrial buildings have replaced older ones and older housing. But there is a clear sign of relative neglect and lack of investment as empty plots of land serve as temporary car parks. Thomas Street itself, or what's left of it, has no visible addresses for housing or business currently being used on it.

The Moore Street electricity substation just south west of Eye Witness Works is of a design so ugly and brutalist that fifty years later the architect is hopefully still doing time for GBH to the environment. It looks like it was designed by the kind of person whose idea of interior design would be to plaster artex on the Sistine Chapel ceiling. The people in the flats opposite must have constant optic nerve damage. Equally philistine was the ugly concrete box of Castle Market built around the same time on the other side of the city centre right on top of the ruins of Sheffield Castle and now knocked down. Only one of these two demolished buildings will be missed. It is easy to imagine that Mao's Cultural Revolution had spread to Sheffield City Council in the 1960s.

North of Egerton Street first a 1960s estate and then a 1990s estate has changed the landscape. Where this estate now stands Bath Street has disappeared and a maze of paths cuts across where it stood. Despite these changes Orwell would still recognise more pockets of Broomhall west of Fitzwilliam Street than east especially closer to the Binns' old home. He would certainly recognise the feel of deprivation.

Today old slum working class areas of Broomhall and other areas of former back-to-back housing are being turned back into residential areas but now aimed at students and the young professional, as well as the occasional older person, of course. The housing that was built from 1919 under the housing acts passed in the two decades after the First World War to rehouse people moved out of the slums, was built, as Orwell saw and noted, away from the town and city centres i.e. in the suburbs. These were the great, formative years of municipal socialism in Sheffield when, in the days when its members were innovators rather than just administrators, the council began to build the great estates of Wybourn, Manor, Arbourthorne, Parson Cross and others. At one point, Parson Cross alone housed 50,000 people or a tenth of the then entire city's population and formed part of Europe's largest social housing concentration.

This isn't Sheffield's only European housing record. In chapter IV Orwell prophetically saw a future other than large suburban housing estates to avoid people being moved out of inner-city areas. *"The simplest solution is flats. If people are going to live in large towns at all they must learn to live on top of one another. But the northern working people do not take kindly to flats; even where flats exist they are contemptuously named 'tenements'. Almost everyone will tell you that he 'wants a house of his own', and apparently a house in the middle of an unbroken block of houses a hundred yards long seems to them more 'their own' than a flat situated in mid-air. "*

Sheffield's first council housing had been such tenements at Townhead. They're still standing over a hundred years later. Decades after they were built however, other new flats that were built elsewhere in Sheffield years after Orwell's visit and along Orwell's recommendations did not meet with the same success.

The Park Hill flats on the hill behind Sheffield Midland Station is Europe's largest listed building, a snaking complex of interlinked blocks of nearly a thousand flats built in the 1950s on the site of rows of demolished inner-city slums, replaced by modern streets in the sky, and officially opened by the then Labour leader Hugh Gaitskell in 1961. Partly based on designs by Le Corbusier, Park Hill was as bold a futuristic attempt at housing as Sheffield's municipal socialism could manage during its heyday. You can't imagine Tony Blair in future years ever having anything to do with anything so municipal or socialist.

It started to go wrong not too long after but the council persevered with the idea and shortly after built other such complexes including Hyde Park flats nearby, the Broomhall flats at the north end of Thomas Street and Kelvin flats, a concrete monstrosity of nearly 1,000 flats, just south of Hillsborough on the opposite side of the Upper Don Valley from where Orwell stayed. If he had lived long enough to return to Parkwood Springs and see Kelvin he would definitely have changed his mind about flats. Some of Parkwood Springs' residents would move there as well as to other areas. However, soon people no longer wanted to live in them so blighted had they become in just a few years. Kelvin was demolished within 30 years of opening. Hyde Park was partly demolished and the rest was refurbished in the early 1990s and survives. So, does Park Hill, albeit now also partially demolished, and is being refurbished by a private company, with its European record intact as it is slowly but gradually made habitable for people who would never have lived there when it was first built.

The crude statistics are that between the end of the war and 1991 Sheffield built over 100,000 new homes and demolished just over half that figure. At one point, before the 1980 Housing Act began to reduce the number of council properties through the right to buy scheme, Sheffield City Council owned 90,000 homes, or 45% of the city's entire housing stock.

Despite some bad reputations (Sheffield 5, the entire S5 postcode in north Sheffield area that includes Parson Cross and Shiregreen, is synonymous among some for somewhere you wouldn't want to live although that should be put into context of the size of the area, as nowhere so large can be free of the problems some parts of it suffer from) the housing estates that Sheffield's municipal socialism built from the 1930s onwards still today provide the bedrock of Labour support in the city. When Labour's political opponents talk of areas where people would vote for a donkey with a red rosette and where they weigh the Labour vote rather than count it they are talking of wards like Manor Castle, Park & Arbourthorne, Shiregreen & Brightside, Southey and Firth Park, and constituencies like Brightside & Hillsborough. Labour built the areas and the areas still build Labour.

These sprawling estates (Wordsworth Avenue in S5 which starts close to Joseph Locke's Wardsend Viaduct, is about two miles long or two thirds the length of the M606 motorway in West Yorkshire) transformed the geography, demography and housing of Sheffield. Orwell, in the diary notes that he typed up for March 3rd at 154 Wallace Road, wrote of the impression that his guide round Sheffield, William Brown, gave him. *"Sheffield is held to lead London in everything, eg. on the one hand the new housing schemes in Sheffield are immensely superior, and on the other hand the Sheffield slums are more squalid than anything London can show"*. Brown wasn't wrong about the superiority of the scale of the housing.

Orwell himself was less enamoured than Brown of Sheffield's municipal socialism in the housing field. A day later he wrote *"The town is being*

24

torn down and rebuilt at an immense speed. Everywhere among the slums are gaps with squalid mounds of bricks where condemned houses have been demolished and on all the outskirts of the town new estates of Corporation houses are going up. These are much inferior, at any rate in appearance, to those at Liverpool. They are in terribly bleak situations, too. One estate just behind where I am living now, at the very summit of a hill, on horrible sticky clay soil and swept by icy winds. Notice that the people going into these new houses from the slums will always be paying higher rents, and also will have to spend much more on fuel to keep themselves warm. Also, in many cases, will be further from their work and therefore spend more on conveyances". The estate at the summit of the hill behind him was Shirecliffe. And he was lucky if he didn't feel the icy winds just about anywhere in Sheffield in March. At least the knowledge he picked up in Sheffield about England's spring weather led him to start a future book on a bright cold day in April

In chapter IV Orwell also admits he knows little of local government finance, in other words the post-First World War housing legislation, and contradicts his observation that Sheffield is being torn down and rebuilt at immense speed by stating *"I merely record the fact that houses are desperately needed and are being built, on the whole, with paralytic slowness".* Admittedly Orwell was talking generally and not just of Sheffield and he spent just three days there but it should have been apparent to him that the city was on a massive program of house-building. In fact, Sheffield was building homes at a speed faster than any other British city and at twice the national rate.

He compounds this with an amazingly inaccurate judgement; *"On balance, the Corporation Estates are better than the slums; but only by a small margin".* Given the contempt he rightfully had for the back-to-backs it is inexplicable that Orwell may have thought the new estates would be only marginally better. They may have their problems but they are a world away from the inner-city slums that Orwell rightly condemned as being unfit for human habitation. The new estates were built on a population density much lower than the back-to-backs, just twelve houses per acre. Twelve back to back houses would have fitted into one of the new estate's house's garden. However, after World War Two this standard was overturned as new homes were not being built in sufficient numbers to meet need following destruction from bombing.

25

For example, thirty years after Sheffield began its mass building of houses it began a mass building of estates dominated by flats as Orwell had advocated. From the late 1950s to the mid-1960s Sheffield undertook the building of flats on such a scale and in such a way that there is an actually a Wikipedia entry called "List of brutalist apartment blocks in Sheffield" that lists many of them. Hanover House, a sixteen-story structure, is the nearest block to Thomas Street listed on it, just a couple of minutes' walk west from where the Binns lived. It is now part of an estate built of predominantly low-rise blocks on the site of old back-to-back streets around what were the western ends of Hodgson Street, Moore Street and Milton Street. Clarence Street which ran north-south across them was bulldozed as well to make way for the inner-city ring road.

Hanover House, which had its cladding removed after the Grenfell disaster, overlooks the ring road with numerous low-rise blocks behind it. Its population density exacerbates the social problems it has. This is merely an anecdote but the only person I know who has lived on the estate only ever goes into Waitrose opposite to get his daily methadone. Other blocks in Sheffield similar to it have already been demolished. The rate of attrition of blocks of flats in Sheffield has been far higher than that of houses. Of course, it can be argued that the design of the blocks is much to blame. New blocks of flats built in recent years in Broomhall have a far greater chance of long-term survival although they are aimed at a different demography than social housing. They have all been built by the private sector. Thanks to national and local government preferences, Sheffield City Council is no longer known for building houses, rather for cutting down trees.

Down the hill from Orwell's windy Shirecliffe, Parkwood Springs was a 19th century railway community built to house workers building and working on the rail lines. Gilbert Searle was an unemployed storekeeper in 1936 but between his house and the end of the street fifteen or so houses away, no fewer than three engine drivers and one other railwayman lived. There was a similar concentration on the opposite side of the road which backed on to the Woodhead line just south of Neepsend Station. Douglas Road was the entry to and exit from Parkwood Springs at the southern end of Wallace Road and the station pedestrian bridge was the northern entrance and exit at the top of Wallace Road. On the other side of the bridge and railway line was the industrial and residential area of Neepsend, dominated on Parkwood Road by the gas works which Orwell was referring to among others when he spoke of *"gaso-meters of another industrial town"* about his arrival in Sheffield by train.

Like the area north of the Wicker, Neepsend was an area dominated by heavy industry. Besides the gas works sandwiched between Parkwood Road and Neepsend Lane there were industrial mills and factories built along the Upper Don Valley down to Kelham Island. Railway sidings just south of Neepsend Station below Wallace Road completed the industrial picture. Opposite the Neepsend railway bridge there were two residential roads, Farfield Road and Hoyland Road, as well as housing on Parkwood Road and other streets.

It was from this base that Orwell travelled by foot and tram on Neepsend Lane to see the industry and slums of 1936 Sheffield. Other than in parts of the city centre it would have been possible for him to spend two days seeing nothing but heavy industry and Victorian housing. After all he wasn't in town to see the many open spaces and Peak District on the western side of the city even if he could have seen them through the smoke. Given the fact that heavy industry and slum housing so dominated all the parts of the city that he visited to the extent that Orwell doesn't acknowledge having had the time to even learn of the existence of any of the mining areas, it's hardly surprising that the overwhelming impression he took away with him is the most negative he could have.

After three days Orwell left Sheffield for Leeds on the morning of Thursday 5th March to stay with his sister Marjorie and brother-in-law Humphrey in the relatively genteel climes of Headingley where he took time out from suffering the industrial pollution of South Yorkshire in order to enjoy the peace and quiet and fresh air of Haworth and the moors. The memories he took with him of his hosts in Sheffield though were as positive as his memories of the city were negative. In his diary after leaving them he wrote "*I was quite sorry to leave the Searles. I have seldom met people with more natural decency. They were as kind to me as anyone could possibly be, and I hope and trust they liked me.*" Despite his fondness for them however, he never met the Searles again. Lodger, writer and tourist guide William Brown left Sheffield shortly after and moved to Kent from where he is known to have corresponded with Orwell.

Within a couple of years, the Searles had left Wallace Road. By the start of the war another couple, Polly and Thomas Chadwick, had moved into number 154. If the Searles had read The Road To Wigan Pier they didn't heed its writer's warnings about the interminable vista of factory chimneys or new estates. They moved to run a grocer's shop at 54 Cricket Inn Road on the corner of St John's Road in Hyde Park near Wybourn on the other side of the Woodhead line from where Orwell saw his interminable vista of factory chimneys. From there they could see not only the chimneys back towards Victoria Station to the left across the Woodhead line but also on the opposite side of Cricket Inn Road to the right the abattoir and further along, Nunnery Colliery. No wonder that Orwell never stayed with them again. A couple of years later they moved again to 54 Sedan Street in Burngreave to run another grocer's shop, one of four corner shops in a short street. They seemed to like properties with 54 in the number. Rumours that they later gave up the grocery business to manage Studio 54 in New York are unfounded.

At the start of the war when the Searles were keeping shop in Hyde Park and then Burngreave Orwell himself was also a shopkeeper in Wallington, Hertfordshire where he moved in April 1936 after returning south from his research. Early in the war he wrote Shopkeepers At War but gave up shop-keeping. The Searles carried on and were still at Sedan Street in the late 1940s. Forty years later, in 1990, they were retired and still together celebrated their diamond wedding anniversary by giving an interview entitled *"Orwell memories on a diamond day"* to the Sheffield Telegraph in which they spoke of Orwell over fifty years after they hosted him and forty years after the writer's death. Gilbert was now a non-residential Chelsea Pensioner. He received a war pension for his military service prior to Orwell's visit. As Orwell noted in his diary; "*Of course I got their whole life-history from them by degrees. Searle is 33 and was an only child. When a youth he joined the Army and was in the Ordnance Corps (or whatever it is called) with the army of occupation in Palestine and in Egypt. He has vivid memories of Egypt and wishes he was back there*".

The last people registered at 154 Wallace Road were Ivy and James Outram in 1972-3. By then Sheffield City Council had ordered the destruction of all the housing on Parkwood Springs as part of a program of slum-clearance under the Housing Act 1957 which set new standards of lighting, heating, hot water and toilets in old Victorian terraced houses. Sedan Street in Burngreave where the Searles lived in the 1940s was demolished at the same time. By coincidence John Grocock of the haulage company fame in Worthing Road lived nearby in Burngreave and like the Searles had a corner shop there, on the corner of Ellsmere Road and Clun Road, which displayed his name at least into the 1960s.

Part of Parkwood Springs had been bombed during the Sheffield blitz of December 1940 as the Luftwaffe targeted industrial sites all along the Don Valley from Hillsborough through to Tinsley, the same areas Orwell had visited, as well as the city centre and suburbs largely on the south side of the city. The German code word for it was Schmelztiegelor, meaning Crucible. Who said the Nazis didn't have a sense of humour? The south end of Wallace Road above the railway sidings saw houses demolished on both sides by bombs and the Methodist chapel at the corner of Pickering Road and Wallace Road was also hit as German planes targeted Neepsend Gas Works, Neepsend Brick Works and industrial units at Kelham Island. Firefighters pumped water out of the Don to put out fires. Whether the chemicals in the yellow water helped or hindered this process isn't known.

By coincidence, the log of a Lufwaffe navigator, Emil Sperle, noted that on the approach to Sheffield from the south, having set off from northern France, out of the plane window he could see snow on the hills to the left, the west, as Orwell had seen himself nearly five years earlier from his train window when approaching Sheffield and noted in his diary entry for March 2nd (*"Thick snow everywhere on the hills as I came along"*). Orwell mentions the same at the end of chapter I of the book. About the December 12th 1940 air-raid Sperle wrote *"There is Sheffield. It is so bright I can make out the course of the rivers. Snow lies on the mountains to the left"*. Two people wrote of their own respective impressions of approaching Sheffield five years apart, one from a train on his way to write about Sheffield's industry and the other from a plane on his way to destroy it.

From one Luftwaffe plane Wicker Arches by Victoria Station took a direct hit although the bomb didn't explode as it passed through the structure down to the pavement. The damage on the underside of the arch is still visible. In an unintended act of solidarity with Sheffield on the part of Orwell, a wartime German air-raid over London destroyed copies of the second edition of The Road To Wigan Pier and another destroyed Orwell's flat. They really were all in it together back then.

Also, in 1940 Neepsend Station closed due to falling use. Thirty years later the Woodhead line was closed to passenger trains between Manchester and Sheffield in favour of the Hope Valley line despite Woodhead being the only one to have been electrified, in the 1950s. In 1981 the Woodhead line closed to freight too as usage fell, even before the 1984-5 miners' strike. Freight trains still run today on a single track between Woodburn Junction and Deepcar and to and from there on a separate short branch to the steelworks at Stocksbridge. The part between Deepcar in Sheffield and Dunford Bridge in Barnsley has had its tracks lifted and is now part of the Trans-Pennine Trail. This includes the later Thurgoland tunnel, the older one having been sealed, and follows the former rail line faithfully although the Stocksbridge road bypass was built across it. Part of the Penistone to Wath section, east from Silkstone Common, is now the Dove Valley Trail.

All the stations east of the Pennines have closed other than Penistone which is on the Sheffield to Huddersfield line via Barnsley although some former railway buildings at other stations still exist, many having become private homes. Penistone Station now has just two platforms, the old Woodhead platform having gone. Where it was, is easily identifiable, between the Trans-Pennine Trail and the Huddersfield-bound platform. Until 1983 trains ran between Sheffield and Penistone on the former Woodhead line as part of the Huddersfield service but these were then rerouted via Barnsley. Football specials used Wadsley Bridge to ferry fans to and from Hillsborough for a few years into the 1990s. The Worsbrough branch from Penistone to Wath branch closed even when there were still functioning coalfields left to serve. On the west side of the Pennines however trains still run on what was the Woodhead line from Manchester Piccadilly to termini at Hadfield and Glossop in Derbyshire.

As one form of transport and one of housing came to an end in Parkwood Springs so another developed in the ruins of a destroyed community. In chapter IV Orwell wrote "*Anyone who wants to see the effects of the housing shortage at their very worse should visit the dreadful caravan-dwellings that exist in numbers in many of the northern towns*". Today a caravan community has moved onto Parkwood

Springs just above the railway line where Wallace Road and Parkwood Road used to be. It is likely that the living conditions there today are as dreadful as Orwell described them elsewhere over eighty years ago. Otherwise a few factories remain but the ski-village built where houses used to be has closed. In an effort to rekindle the spirit of the blitz it gets targeted by arsonists every now and again.

In a nice twist of fate, the preparations for the levelling of the housing on Parkwood Springs were filmed in 1974 as a background to the film Slade In Flame. For unexplained reasons of artistic licence the Wolverhampton band became a partly-Sheffield band and various scenes were filmed on both sides of the Upper Don Valley in Walkley, Hillsborough and Parkwood Springs. After thirty and fifty-three minutes there are scenes of the boarded-up houses on Douglas Road, with the gasometers of Neepsend Gas Works in the background in the latter scene. Kelvin flats, built on the Park Hill model, on the other side of the valley also feature in other scenes. Drummer Don Powell lived there in the film and worked in a steel factory. In real life he had actually worked in an iron foundry so that bit wasn't that far, far away from real life. Kelvin flats were demolished nearly twenty years later, long after glam rock had gone out of fashion. Kelvin also featured in Ken Loach's Looks And Smiles, made in 1981, as did Hyde Park flats purely to highlight the depravation of the time. It should be noted that Kelvin was chosen as the most depressing background in Ken Loach's most depressing film.

After the demolitions Parkwood Springs featured almost inevitably in the Full Monty along with most of the rest of Sheffield. Before then, in 1963, The Children's Film Foundation made Wings Of Mystery with scenes filmed on Parkwood Springs about child detectives looking for a secret alloy stolen from a laboratory. It happened a lot back then.

Stranger still was a 1968 Italian film called La Ragaza Con Pistola (The Girl With The Pistol) which made its way from Sicily to Swinging Parkwood Springs where after 38 minutes Monica Vitti and Tony Booth, getting a lot closer to the urban working class than his future son-in-law ever would, descend the steps leading from Wallace Road to Neepsend railway bridge with part of Wallace Road visible behind them i.e. the same route Orwell would have taken thirty years earlier. In the background on the other side of the line are the houses of Farfield Road running down the side of Neepsend Gas Works. The film was nominated for an Oscar for Best Foreign Language Film in 1969 but lost out to the Soviet production of War And Peace presumably on the grounds that the horrors of the Napoleonic Wars were more family-friendly than Neepsend Gas Works.

After March 1936 Orwell never returned to Parkwood Springs. He had seen enough of the chimneys, sulphur, pollution, slums, factories, furnaces and mills of steelmaking Sheffield and after a week's recuperation with family in Leeds would head for the final destination of his research for what would become The Road To Wigan Pier. Following recommendations that he received in Wigan he was to return to a mining community. He then moved to Wallington in Hertfordshire where he would spend much of the rest of 1936 writing his research up into a book that would be published the following year. By the end of 1936, after handing in the book's typed script for publication, Orwell would be on his way to Spain to fight Franco's nationalist forces. Before Barcelona however came Barnsley.

Parkwood Springs (left) and Neepsend (middle and right) separated by the Woodhead line.

Parkwood Springs is the housing area on the left. Wallace Road is the rightmost road curving up the photo immediately to the left of the railway line, the Woodhead line. Orwell lodged in the second row from the rail line, the house being out of shot to the left.

The Woodhead line separates Parkwood Springs from Neepsend. Neepsend Station is also just out of shot to the left. The passenger bridge at the station linked the end of Wallace Road to Parkwood Road in the bottom left of the picture at the ends of the two residential roads which run left to right across the bottom, Farfield Road and Hoyland Road. Above them are Neepsend Gas Works, with houses on Parkwood Road between the gasometers. The road running up the right-hand side is Neepsend Lane where trams are visible where Orwell travelled by tram during his stay there. The curve of the Don is visible to the right of Neepsend Lane towards the top of the picture. Also at the top of the picture industry stretches towards Kelham Island and Attercliffe along the Don Valley

33

Orwell's *"frightful patch of waste ground"*.

The patch of land that Orwell describes in chapter VII as a *"frightful patch of waste ground"* is the triangular piece of land in the middle of the photo about a third of the way down from the top, just to the right of the white smoke. The bottom right tip of the waste ground is the junction of Worthing Road (top) and Lumley Street (below and up the right of the waste land) where the road bends. It now has factories on it. Orwell would have stood on this land looking across Worthing Road at the cubicle yellow and brown building, one of the industrial buildings to the left, which is partially obscured by the smoke. To his right at the top of the photo is the *"isolated row of gaunt four-roomed houses,"* the short row of half a dozen or so white (or as white as they could be in that location) houses on Lovetot Road. Only the left hand one on the corner of Worthing Road and Lovetot Road, the Woodbourne Hotel, survives. All the rest of the housing above Lovetot Road on Woodbourn Hill, Woodbourn Road and Ripon Street has been cleared and the area is no longer a residential one. Woodbourn Road is the long road that runs across from top right across the railway line where it becomes

34

residential. Woodbourn Road tram stop now stands where some of the houses pictured stood on the left.

Immediately to the left of the block of industrial buildings on Worthing Road under the smoke runs the Sheffield Tinsley Canal. To its left is Effingham Road and then the river Don. The road running up the bottom left hand side is Attercliffe Road. Behind Orwell, to the right of the waste ground, was the railway embankment of the Woodhead line. Almost all of these tracks have been lifted and replaced by a new waste ground. The few remaining tracks serve the Sheffield to Lincoln line and industrial use. The white marks in the top right hand corner are not the result of a nuclear accident but are part of Nunnery Colliery.

The "*interminable vista of factory chimneys*" that Orwell would have seen to his left are out of shot below.

Orwell's *"interminable vista of factory chimneys"*.

The bottom tip of the waste ground, the junction of Worthing Road and Lumley Street, on which Orwell stood, is in the very top left corner of the photo. Lumley Street runs down with the Woodhead line running parallel immediately above it. The white smoke blows over the railway lines.

The building on the right of the photo is Sheffield Victoria Station, the passenger terminal of the Woodhead line. The tracks carry on round to the left and run behind the waste ground. At the bottom of the station are the Wicker Arches and flowing from right to left by them is the river Don. Above and below the Don is the *"interminable vista of factory chimneys"*. Roads shown above it include Effingham Street, Effingham Road, Foley Street, Leveson Street, Sussex Road and Sussex Street. Effingam Street Gas Works and some residential homes are also shown to the left of Victoria Station. Savile Street runs across the picture below the Don with Attercliffe Road running into it from the left.

Below Saville Street is Wicker Station and below that more homes and factories round Spital Hill and Carlisle Street.

In the top right hand corner of the photo are houses in Hyde Park to where Orwell's hosts Kate and Gilbert Searle moved from Parkwood Springs a few years after his stay. He didn't return to enjoy the view.

Thomas Street, Broomhall

The junction of Egerton Street (left) and Thomas Street (right). 13/2 Thomas Street was about 150 yards down on the left.

Barnsley

After a month of working class life in Lancashire George Orwell had a week's break in Headingley in Leeds, staying with his sister and brother-in-law and generally doing what the working classes he had just spent time with couldn't afford to do, visiting the Brontes' former home in Haworth and relaxing in a cottage at Middlesmoor on the moors. On Thursday 12th March 1936 he travelled the twenty or so miles south to Barnsley. After the smoke, chimneys, serrated flames, railways, gas, steam hammers, sulphur and watching the river glow in Sheffield he was back in a mining area following recommendations he received among the mines of Wigan. He initially wasn't planning on staying long as his expectations were low. On settling in at his lodgings he wasn't confident that Barnsley would give him much material for the book. However, he stayed for just over two weeks, almost as long as he stayed in Wigan and possibly equally as long.

After two weeks of staying in Wigan, Orwell had travelled to Liverpool to stay with Mary and John Deiner who were members of the Adelphi literary circle of which Orwell was part. In his diary entry for February 27th about his stay there Orwell wrote that he stayed just the one night (Wednesday 25th) there before returning to Wigan on the evening of the following day, presumably Thursday. Orwell was wrong in at least one respect here as the Wednesday of that week was the 26th not the 25th and in 1970 Mary Deiner gave an interview to the BBC for an Omnibus program about Orwell in which she claimed that when Orwell turned up in Liverpool he was so ill, possibly from bronchitis, that he collapsed and had to convalesce in bed for a few days until he was well enough to be driven round Liverpool before returning to Wigan.

This was a result of Orwell having gone down Bryn Hall Colliery in Ashton-in-Makerfield, the only pit he went down while staying in Wigan. This had been on 23rd February, supervised by Jerry Kennan, an Independent Labour Party member, who claimed on the same Omnibus program that Orwell disappeared for four days afterwards.

Orwell's previous diary entry before Liverpool was for 24th February in Wigan when he mentioned the Bryn Hall Colliery visit and his next one was for 2nd March in Sheffield. Regardless of whether or not Orwell was ill in bed in Liverpool, there are still a few days not accounted for. If he really did return to Wigan on 26th or 27th February there are no diary entries covering the 3 or 4 days from then till March 2nd that he would have spent back in Wigan before he travelled to Sheffield (1936 was a leap year). If he did, as Mary Deiner claimed, spend four or five days in Liverpool he may not have returned to Wigan until February 29th or March 1st.

If this latter case were true then why would Orwell have covered up the length of his illness? And if he really did return when he claimed he had in his diaries then what did he do on the missing three or four days in Wigan? Either he had been ill in Liverpool for a few days and subsequently was covering his illness up for whatever reason, or Deiner's recollections were wrong and a few days are unaccounted for in Wigan. If the former is true and he did spend four or five days in Liverpool then it can be assumed that he stayed about the same time in Barnsley as he had in Wigan, just over a fortnight.

There is an old Monty Python sketch called Working Class Playwright which sends up the 1960s social development of working class offspring going off to university and becoming estranged from their roots. Its relevance to Orwell's time in Barnsley becomes greater the more you find out about the writer's stay there. If you haven't seen it I'll not spoil it but the key line is "*Hampstead wasn't good enough for you. You had to go poncing off to Barnsley*".

By coincidence Orwell had just a couple of months earlier given up his part-time job in a bookshop, Booklover's Corner, on the corner of Pond Street and South End Green in Hampstead in order to travel north to do research for The Road To Wigan Pier. On March 12th he was lodging at 4 Agnes Terrace in Barnsley, a short row of seven houses, which, as it happens, runs between Day Street and Barnsley's Pond Street. This, other than by name, predictably bears little resemblance to its NW3 namesake. The people of Barnsley would have it no other way after all and no doubt so would the people of Hampstead. Orwell had also lived on the Hampstead Pond Street till just over twelve months earlier. And by another coincidence the Pond Street in Barnsley, in a way that the one in Hampstead was never likely to be, was right on the edge of a large slum clearance area that Orwell was going to look round when researching the housing problems of the town.

Other than his lodgings at 4 Agnes Terrace it didn't start well. After a couple of days Orwell wrote in his diary entry for March 14th "*I am very comfortable in this house but do not think I shall pick up much of interest in Barnsley. I know no one here except Wilde, who is thoroughly vague. Cannot discover whether there is a branch of the N.U.W.M. here. The public library is no good. There is no proper reference library and it seems no separate directory of Barnsley is published.*"

Wilde was Herbert Wilde, a director of the Barnsley British Co-operative Society, chairman of his local Monk Bretton cricket club and the secretary of the South Yorkshire Branch of the Working Men's Club & Institute Union whose social evening Orwell attended that day on Wellington Street at the then Radical and Liberal Club. This is now Wellington House and by another coincidence a temporary home of the public library. Wilde's life seems to have been dedicated to the co-operative cause. Just a month earlier he had travelled to Sheffield to open a concert hall extension to the Manor Estate Social Club on City Road.

Despite the illness Orwell had suffered following his visit to Bryn Hall Colliery, within a day or two he had arranged to go down Grimethorpe pit in Barnsley. He may not have been aware of it but he was actually staying right on top of a disused pit. About twenty yards south from Agnes Terrace, between Pond Street and Day Street, there is the top of a former mine shaft that had been the entrance to Agnes Pit. This had shut about fifty years before Orwell came to Barnsley as it was too far from any railway. In 1936 immediately next to Agnes Terrace was a row of four houses called Agnes Pit Yard in front of which was the former entrance to the pit shaft, marked by what looked like a concrete bunker. Today it is still visible but now is what looks like a large concrete bottle top on the ground just off a public path that runs between Pond Street and Day Street. "*Our civilization, pace Chesterton, is founded on coal...*" he subsequently wrote at the start of chapter 2. Few in 1936 would have had the insight to recognise Wigan and Barnsley as the cradles of civilization.

Parallel to the Agnes Pit entrance no housing had been built on either side of Pond Street and on one side of Day Street, although a building which used to be the Oak Leaf pub on Day Street still stands. The disused Agnes Pit mineshaft is just in its grounds. The council housing that was built to replace the old slums just east of Pond Street have some of the largest gardens any social housing could have. There is a good fifty-yard gap between numbers 10 and 12 Pond Street. The reason is the old Agnes Pit as that is where the pit yard was. I did my paper round up Pond Street and back down Day Street for over four years in the 1970s and never realised there had been a mine there. The houses that were 1 to 4 Agnes Pit Yard have been demolished.

Agnes Pit may have been closed by then but in Britain in 1936 nearly 2,000 other pits employed over three quarters of a million men in mining, although that figure was down by nearly half a million compared to twenty years previously. Like in Wigan, Orwell soon got busy with exploring the conditions of the miners. Despite having been so close to Nunnery Colliery while in Sheffield he doesn't seem to have paid any attention to any of the mines that were there at the time, presumably due to his preoccupation in the limited time he spent there with housing and the overall environmental impact of the factories, mills and gas works of the city. By another coincidence where he had lodged in Sheffield had also been the site of another disused colliery, Parkwood, which had been dug horizontally off Parkwood Road into the Parkwood Springs hillside to mine ganister and coal between 1916 and 1920.

Sheffield's mines were generally concentrated in the east and south east of the city and were dug along several Yorkshire coalfield seams including the two most important, Barnsley and Parkgate, as well as others such as Silkstone and High Hazel. They stretched from Tinsley and Nunnery east of the city centre southwards through Catcliffe, Orgreave, Handsworth, Beighton, Birley and down towards Kiverton Park and Nottinghamshire. Others were sunk on the same seams just over the boundary in Rotherham. One thought. If he had indeed explored the mines in this area would he have called the book Homage To Catcliffe? Let's move on.

Before rail nationalisation in 1948 all Sheffield's mines in this area were on or linked to the rail lines of the London and North Eastern Railway (previously the Manchester, Sheffield and Lincolnshire Railway until 1897 and from then until 1923 the Great Central Railway) and as such were served by rail links of the Woodhead line to Rotherwood sidings and from there by an extension towards Nottinghamshire and Lincolnshire. Handsworth Colliery was the last mine to close in

Sheffield in 1968 when it became exhausted. Both Nunnery and East Birley had closed either during the war or after. Other nearby pits on the same seams but over the boundary in Rotherham survived longer. Orgreave closed in 1981, Brookhouse Beighton in 1985, Kiveton Park in 1994 and Silverwood the following year. Orwell had been close to mines in Sheffield but hadn't chosen to explore them.

In Barnsley he was well-lodged both for his exploration of work in the mines and of living conditions in the back-to-back slums. His hosts for his two-week stay were a mining family, Albert Gray, who had fought in World War One and been invalided out with a leg injury, and Minnie Gray and their two daughters, Irene and Doreen. Nearly fifty years later the then Irene Goodliffe gave an interview to the BBC for an Arena documentary on Orwell's stay. She was still living in 4 Agnes Terrace, then with her husband Kenneth. In 1936 her father Albert was a miner who worked in Darton, four miles north of the town, possibly at North Gawber pit in Mapplewell near to where Orwell visited at least twice to see both the mining homes next to the pit and the working conditions above ground. Other pits in Darton were Wooley and Darton Main.

In chapter 10 Orwell wrote; "*Via Socialist politics you can get in touch with the working-class intelligentsia, but they are hardly more typical than tramps or burglars. For the rest you can only mingle with the working class by staying in their houses as a lodger, which always has a dangerous resemblance to slumming'. For some months I lived entirely in coal-miners' houses.*" Ignoring the fact that the house he lodged at in Sheffield wasn't a miner's home, the working-class intelligentsia he was referring to were William Brown in Sheffield and Herbert Wilde in Barnsley, who Orwell had been put in touch with through Adelphi and neither of whom he seemed to get on with.

Also in chapter 10 he wrote; "*Literary London now teems with young men who are of proletarian origin and have been educated by means of scholarships. Many of them are very disagreeable people, quite unrepresentative of their class, and it is most unfortunate that when a person of bourgeois origin does succeed in meeting a proletarian face to face on equal terms, this is the type he most commonly meets. For the result is to drive the bourgeois, who has idealized the proletariat so long as he knew nothing about them, back into frenzies of snobbishness. The process is sometimes very comic to watch, if you happen to be watching it from the outside. The poor well-meaning bourgeois, eager to embrace his proletarian brother, leaps forward with open arms; and only a little while later he is in retreat, minus a borrowed five pounds and exclaiming dolefully, 'But, dash it, the fellow's not a gentleman*!'. Other than predicting the above-mentioned Monty Python sketch by 30 years with its mention of literary London teeming with working class playwrights, this can also be read as a disguised attack on Brown and Wilde as well as Orwell making excuses for his own snobbery towards them

Orwell visited four Barnsley mines in all, going down two of them – Grimethorpe, five miles north east of the town centre and Wentworth Silkstone in Stainborough, three miles west of Barnsley. The latter of these was served by the Worsbrough branch of the Woodhead line from Penistone to Wath that was used to transport coal. Other than North Gawber, the pit that he visited but didn't go down was Barnsley Main just outside the town centre. At North Gawber he also looked at housing in Spring Gardens, a row of back-to-back housing off Pit Lane End, now Blacker Road, just by the pit entrance, which Orwell described in his diary entry for 23rd March as "*Houses about the worst I have seen, though we did not manage to get into the very worst ones, which were one-roomed or two-roomed cabins of stone, about 20' by 15' by 15' high, or even less, and practically ruinous*".

In chapter 4 of the book he writes of the same property "*House in Mapplewell (small mining village near Barnsley). Two up, one down. Living-room 14 ft by 13 ft. Sink in living-room. Plaster cracking and coming off walls. No shelves in oven. Gas leaking slightly. The upstairs rooms each 10 ft by 8 ft. Four beds (for six persons, all adult), but 'one bed does nowt', presumably for lack of bedclothes. Room nearest stairs has no door and stairs have no banister, so that when you step out of bed your foot hangs in vacancy and you may fall ten feet on to stones. Dry rot so bad that one can see through the floor into the room below. Bugs, but 'I keeps 'em down with sheep dip'. Earth road past these cottages is like a muck-heap and said to be almost impassable in winter. Stone lavatories at ends of gardens in semi-ruinous condition. Tenants have been twenty-two years in this house*." It may seem strange that a large family would live in such a three-roomed slum for so long (twenty-two years in this case) but in Spring Gardens there were in 1936 at least four families – the Browns, Pinders, Swanns and Wrights - with at least six adults (one had eight) who had lived there, since at least 1918. The council was building new homes but cases like this underline the size and severity of the problem it had to overcome. And Spring Gardens didn't even have house numbers.

Orwell didn't need to travel the four miles to Mapplewell to see such housing conditions however. Among the papers that he took away with him from Barnsley as part of his research was an article from the Barnsley Chronicle from March 1934, exactly two years before his visit, about the proposed demolition of slum housing right next door to where he was then lodged. This concerned the New Street, Oakwell Yard and Drakes Yard clearance areas and contained a map of the New Street area, roughly bounded by New Street to the north, Sheffield Road to the east, Park Road to the south and Pond Street to the west. Orwell was lodged just yards from Pond Street.

Although the name is not used or even heard of much anymore this part of Barnsley was known as Barebones. A hundred years before Orwell's visit it had been one of the most important areas of Yorkshire's weaving industry, predominantly based in people's cellars, until Barnsley fell behind as factory-based work became established elsewhere. By the second part of the nineteenth century mining was becoming the chief industry in Barnsley and weaving was considered work for women as men dug coal. Both industries are represented, along with glass-making, on the town's coat of arms, weaving by two shuttles.

Some houses were specifically designed for weaving work and known as weavers' cottages. They had half a dozen or so steps coming up off the street so that the ground floor was raised. This allowed the cellar ceiling to be above ground level so that windows could be used for air and light for the cellar, enabling weavers to work there.

In 1936 Barebones had thousands of houses – weavers' cottages, back-to-back and other types. Today only two buildings survive in the entire area from that time, a Methodist church and chapel on what was Buckley Street, next door to one another and dating back to 1869 and 1876. Like Broomhall in Sheffield, Barebones took decades to clear. Some of the old slums still stood as late as the 1960s. New houses, both council and private, were built but again like Sheffield away from the town centre side and nearer to Park Road. These included, as Orwell had called for, a greater concentration of flats than on other council estates in Barnsley. Three blocks of flats stand close to Sheffield Road, Barnsley's only council high-rise.

The parts of Barebones closest to the town centre were reserved for light industrial development. Today much of it resembles the part of Broomhall close to Thomas Street, starved of investment with empty factories and ad hoc car parks. If you walk out of Barnsley town centre along Heelis Street or out of Sheffield city centre on Thomas Street you get the same sense of the areas being abandoned that you hardly get in other parts of Barnsley and Sheffield close to the centres. Housing though has finally returned to this part of Heelis Street with a tall block of modern apartments. It took ten years to build but Orwell's flats march on slowly but surely and in the private sector.

In chapter 4 of The Road To Wigan Pier, Orwell mentions three Barnsley homes he visited - one in Wortley Street in the town centre, one on Peel Street in Worsborough Common and one in Spring Gardens in Mapplewell. Besides these, according to his notes and narrative, he also visited two others in Blucher Street, just round the corner from Wortley Street, one in Albert Street East in the town centre, all on the other side of New Street from Barebones, and another on Providence Street which ran parallel to the top end of Pond Street in the south west corner of Barebones, a hundred yards or so from where Orwell stayed. These were all back-to-back houses. As a bit of counter-balance he also visited a more recent council house on Wilthorpe Crescent a mile west of the town centre. Barnsley had started building new council estates about fifteen years earlier at about the same time as Sheffield, under the new housing legislation of the inter-war years.

The house number in Peel Street isn't specified but it could have been the Cone family at number 43 based on its location and number of adults in the house. There was only one court on the street and the higher numbers (47 was the highest number) fronted it and would have shared an outside toilet, or privy midden, with its occupants. In his notes Orwell gave house numbers for other homes he visited. The occupants of 23 Blucher Street were Alice and Edward Williams, and of 27 Blucher Street, Elizabeth and Charles Shaw, John McNally and Harriet Cooper. The

45

latter was considered the best house in the street. To put this in context the residents had to share an outside toilet with ten other houses. And like all the back-to-back houses of Barebones a short walk away on the other side of New Street they were slums that were cleared in the years to come under the same legislation that Sheffield used to clear its slums. Barnsley Council however also had the foresight to photograph some of them before they were demolished. These are known as the Bleasby photographs and can be found on the Barnsley Council website. Some are included in this book.

The occupants of 12, Albert Street East, right in the town centre, were Agnes May Firth and Ellis Firth. Orwell first became aware of the latter on his first weekend in Barnsley. There were two major events happening in the town on Saturday 14th and Sunday 15th March. On the Saturday Barnsley FC were trying to avoid relegation from the second tier of English football at home to Nottingham Forest. They lost. Some things never change.

On the Sunday, no doubt regretful at having missed the first event despite its taking place at a ground whose name was the closest of all sporting venues' names to the writer's chosen nom de plume, George Oakwell went to see Oswald Mosley speak at a British Union of Fascists rally in the Public Hall (now Civic Hall) on Eldon Street in the town centre.

It may now seem strange to say but in 1936 fascism didn't have the tarnished reputation it does today. Its proponents still believed and propagated that fascism was a modern, progressive, dynamic and legitimate alternative to liberal democracy. Who says fake news is a recent concept? It hadn't yet had the chance to become a synonym for tens of millions of dead. Orwell however, already and with great foresight knew where he stood with regards to fascism (against if you weren't sure) and so did many others to the extent that not everyone who attended a BUF rally was there to warmly congratulate Mosley for his Jew-baiting, xenophobia, bigotry and all-round demagoguery.

Some attended to point out to him that concentration camps and dictatorship were as surely the inevitable outcomes of Mosley's own political direction as they had become those of Mosley's idol, Adolf Hitler. Mosley, not really open to rational persuasion and determined without intended irony to refute the accusations of importing National Socialist practices from Nazi Germany, employed blackshirts round the hall to convince the doubters through the strong use of gratuitous violence that the BUF really wasn't the same as the NSDAP. He may also have burnt a few books in order to underline his commitment to the principle of freedom of expression. The public library, used for the dirty book scene in Kes, was also in the Public Hall, by which time it had become the Civic Hall.

It was in this atmosphere of political violence that Orwell first saw Ellis Firth who was running across the stage as Mosley spoke. Firth was not trying to interrupt the speaker although that was the impression Mosley got. In his notes Orwell quoted Mosley as saying "*A typical example of Red tactics!*" on seeing Firth being swallowed up by the blackshirts and thrown out of the hall with levels of violence that today would have led to the entire BUF membership being ineligible to gain a bouncer's licence. What Firth was actually trying to do was to come to the assistance of another non-believer who himself was also undergoing an unsolicited physical re-education program meted out by Mosley's private army. Unable to get through the crowd to help the man, Firth decided that the easiest way to get to his friend's aid was to go round the crowd via the stage. If only life were so simple.

Pastor Niemoeller's maxim that first they came for the communists should at this point be turned on its head as first it was the communists who came for them. The man to whose aid Firth was trying to get was Tommy Degnan who just two weeks earlier on Sunday 1st March, a day before Orwell left Wigan for Sheffield, had been in the same hall chairing a Communist Party public meeting on "Working Class Unity" addressed by its leader, Willie Gallacher, then MP for West Fife and the last communist member of parliament. Degnan was originally from Wigan and in 1936 was working at Wharncliffe Woodmoor pit in Carlton, a few miles north of Barnsley town centre. He was at the time off work owing to an accident in the mine but still determined to give as good as he got. He was an active trades-unionist and a few months after the meeting he stood unsuccessfully to be his branch's delegate to the Yorkshire Miners' Association's (YMA's) Area Council. A forerunner of the YMA, the South Yorkshire Miners' Association, had been founded in Barnsley in 1881.

47

Degnan had moved to Barnsley following his brother Ted who had found work there at Barrow Colliery after being unemployed in the aftermath of the 1921 strike. Before then he had been taken prisoner in World War One and forced to work in a Polish mine. He joined the Communist Party in 1922 and remained a member all his life. Frank Watters, a former Scottish miner and the party's industrial organiser who was sent to Yorkshire in 1953 to build communist influence and a cohesive left organisation in the Yorkshire NUM, was warned in advance by the regional party secretary that he would have to get Degnan on his side if he was to have any chance of success, as Degnan was the "*hardest bastard among the bunch of bastards*" that constituted Yorkshire miners. In part two of the book Orwell wrote "*Even with miners who described themselves as Communists I found that it needed tactful manoeuvrings to prevent them from calling me 'sir'; and all of them, except in moments of great animation, softened their northern accents for my benefit*". Degnan's moments of animation probably meant he was one of the exceptions.

At about the same time in the 1950s Degnan met a young miner named Arthur Scargill and mentored him. Both Scargill and Watters spoke at Degnan's funeral at Ardsley Crematorium in Barnsley in 1979. However, Orwell had written Degnan's oblique epitaph over forty years earlier in chapter 11 of The Road To Wigan Pier; "*To the ordinary working man, the sort you would meet in any pub on Saturday night, Socialism does not mean much more than better wages and shorter' hours and nobody bossing you about. To the more revolutionary type, the type who is a hunger-marcher and is blacklisted by employers, the word is a sort of rallying-cry against the forces of oppression, a vague threat of future violence.*" Degnan was the revolutionary type of the second line, having been a hunger-marcher in 1930 and blacklisted by employers because of his militancy. It was Orwell's hidden reference to Degnan, hidden possibly as the author might have been thinking about a threat of future violence, vague or not.

This wasn't the only reference to Degnan without naming him. In 1936 he was living in a squat near the town centre which Orwell visited. In chapter 5 Orwell writes of Degnan's home, although he doesn't name him, which he shared with others and which Orwell visited; "*In one town I remember a whole colony of them who were squatting, more or less illicitly, in a derelict house which was practically falling down. They had collected a few scraps of furniture, presumably off refuse-tips, and I remember that their sole table was an old marble-topped wash-hand-stand"*. At one point, in the mid-1940s, Tommy Degnan lived nearby in a back-to-back on New Street on the edge of Barebones, so his housing conditions didn't improve much over the years.

In the same 1970 Omnibus program that Mary Deiner and Jerry Keenan had appeared in, Degnan recounted that following the Mosley meeting he and Orwell drank together in the Three Cranes Hotel on Queen Street around the corner from the Public Hall and argued over the best tactics to confront the rise of fascism in Britain. Orwell's diaries suggest it was the following day. Predictably Degnan favoured a more confrontational approach and the liberal Orwell a more measured one. Degnan pointed to the case of Nazi Germany where SPD complacency and accommodation of Hitler had failed. Despite their differences both men would be fighting Franco's nationalist forces in Spain within less than a year and because of them each was in a different camp, Orwell in the POUM through the Independent Labour Party and Degnan in the International Brigades though the Communist Party.

What did unite them unfortunately was that both were shot, Orwell in the neck and Degnan in the lower part of his right lung. Degnan, like Orwell, had arrived in Spain in December 1936 and just two months later took a bullet that stayed in him for the next forty-three years until he died in March 1979. Orwell was shot in May 1937, was declared unfit for military service as a result and eventually fled Spain as the Stalinists in the International Brigades sought to persecute the alleged Trotskyists of the POUM.

For the rest of his life Degnan remained both a committed member of the Communist Party, serving for a long time on the National Executive Committee, and trades unionist in the NUM. He often combined the two by selling the Morning Star at NUM meetings. He continued to live and work in Barnsley but his International Brigades service was also recognised in his birth place of Wigan. A commemorative plaque was unveiled in April 2018 at Southside Gardens in Wigan town centre in honour of Degnan and eleven others who had fought against Franco in Spain. A similar memorial had been unveiled in Barnsley in the St Mary's Church memorial garden in Church Street in the town centre in 2006 in commemoration of those from Barnsley who fought there.

They're not named on the memorial but were William Brent, John Hallworth, Harold Horbury, Norman Mason, Stephen Ward and Tommy Degnan.

In his diary notes Orwell wrote that he thought Degnan had been charged under the Public Meetings Act, as Mosley had threatened to anyone thrown out with a promise of a £5 and prison sentence on top. In fact, there is evidence that only two people were charged with offences arising from the meeting, neither being Degnan and neither for anything that happened in the hall. Orwell mentions them in a diary entry a week later when a collection was held for them at a communist street meeting in Barnsley town centre. They were Norman Stanley, aged 20, of Worsborough Dale and John Hobson, aged 18, of Bridge Street who were each fined £2 including costs with a £5 surety and bound over for six months for another £5. Their offences were committed just behind the Public Hall, on the corner of Eastgate and Regent Street and involved using bricks and stones to smash the windows of the coaches which had brought and were taking home the BUF supporters who had been bussed in for the event. So money well spent.

The cost of the damage inside the hall amounted to 12 shillings. There couldn't have been much left of the building. Barnsley council subsequently banned the BUF from holding meetings there again and the Barnsley ban was used by the authorities in Hull as a reason to ban the BUF from there. On the plus side for Mosley at least he was spared an evening in Hull. Mosley indirectly got his own back on Barnsley when the BUF's behaviour led to the government passing The Public Order Act 1936 which fifty years later was used extensively against flying pickets during the 1984-5 miners' strike.

Degnan's street credibility may have been insulted by not being charged with starting World War II three and a half years early but he made up for it in other ways. Despite being a miner, he was active in the National Unemployed Workers Movement (NUWM), set up by the Communist Party in 1921, which arranged communist speakers as well as other activities for the unemployed. It also organised hunger marches of the 1920s and 1930s. Degnan had taken part in the 1930 one. Orwell had been in touch with the NUWM in Wigan where Paddy Grady had recommended that Orwell get in touch with Degnan in Barnsley. It was by coincidence that Orwell had seen Degnan getting thrown out of the

Mosley meeting. Orwell mentions the NUWM in chapter 6 of The Road To Wigan Pier as well as the official centres for unemployed people. Orwell visited the one in Barnsley, the Unemployment Occupational Centre (run by the council's Social Services department), which was based at Milton House on Wellington Street and was an all-male affair organising classes in such as woodworking, weaving and upholstering. He observed that the main activity in the NUWM one was dominoes and that it needed other occupational activities if it was to match the official one.

What Degnan thought of such activities can be guessed at by the fact that his rival work for the NUWM was intended as a direct political alternative to the council's unemployed services. Degnan not only organised communist speakers for the NUWM but also for the town centre street meetings, probably on May Day Green or at the bottom of Market Hill. In his notes Orwell wrote *"Communist meeting in the Market Place disappointing. The trouble with all these Communist speakers is that instead of using the popular idiom they employ immensely long sentences full of "despite" and "notwithstanding" and "be that as it may" etc. in the Garvin strain – and this in spite of always speaking with broad provincial or cockney accents – Yorkshire in this case. I suppose they are given set speeches which they learn by heart. After the visiting speaker Degnan got up to speak and was a much more effective speaker – he speaks very broad Lancashire and though he can talk like a leading article if he wants to he doesn't choose. The usual crowd of men of all ages gaping with entirely expressionless faces and the usual handful of women a little more animated then the men – I suppose because no woman would go to a political meeting unless exceptionally interested in politics. About 150 people. Collection take for the defence of the young men arrested in the Mosley affair and realised 6/-".* He also wrote a similar paragraph in chapter 11 without naming Degnan, just before the above unnamed reference to a vague threat of future violence. Much of chapter 11 is an uncredited homage to Degnan.

As in Wigan, Orwell also visited the coal face while in Barnsley. His two days down the *"day hole,"* of the mines of Barnsley were on 19th March at Wentworth Silkstone pit in Stainborough and two days later at Grimethorpe pit. After the former visit he wrote in his diary of walking the two miles up the hill to Dodworth to get the bus back into Barnsley.

Don't let anyone tell you that the life of the writer is not one of romance and adventure.

On the March 22nd he visited but didn't go down Barnsley Main where Degnan had worked before the 1926 strike, just a couple of miles east of the town centre, and on the 23rd and 25th March he did likewise at North Gawber, also visiting houses at Spring Gardens there at the same time. Bearing in mind that the pits in 1936 were privately owned and in need of investment especially with regards to safety, in chapter 3 he wrote of the dangers of mining; " T*he rate of accidents among miners is so high, compared with that in other trades, that casualties are taken for granted almost as they would be in a minor war. Every year one miner in about nine hundred is killed and one in about six is injured;"* and "*The most obviously understandable cause of accidents is explosions of gas, which is always more or less present in the atmosphere of the pit*".

In 1935 171 men were killed in Yorkshire mines alone, up from 107 the previous year. Just ten years later the post-war Labour government passed the Coal Industry Nationalisation Act 1946. Improved health and safety had been a big incentive for the miners to call for nationalisation. In areas like Barnsley mining was a way of life as much as a profession. When I was thirteen a friend's brother in law remarked that the miners had the worst jobs in the world but would fight for them harder than anyone else. It was a paradox but echoed Orwell's point above, that the dangers of mining were an accepted part of the work even if one that the miners sought to have minimised as much as possible.

In 1866 Barnsley Main, then called Oaks Colliery, had been the scene of England's worst ever mining tragedy when over 360 men were killed by a series of explosions. Further disasters happened there in the 1940s. And just six months before Orwell's visit to North Gawber pit, in September 1935, nineteen men had been killed there, including one resident of Spring Gardens, by an explosion. The next such disaster in Barnsley happened just over four months after Orwell had left, at Wharncliffe Woodmoor pit in Carlton, Tommy Degnan's colliery, when fifty-eight miners died. Even though Lloyd George had promised a land fit for heroes of World War I, those who had returned from fighting in World War I, like Tommy Degnan and Albert Gray, were still having to work in appalling danger. Despite such disasters being national news and the Wharncliffe Woodmoor disaster happening at the time when Orwell was writing the book, he made no mention of it to underline the dangers of mining that he was writing about.

As Orwell judged Barnsley in March 1936 so Barnsley reciprocated exactly a year later. In a review of The Road To Wigan Pier on its publication the Barnsley Chronicle's editor, Gilbert Langstaff gave the book an overall positive though sometimes critical welcome in a language unusually flowery for the Barnsley of 1937, or of any time for that matter. The criticism was reserved for the book's factual inaccuracies as well as for comments about the new Town Hall and the town's Unemployment Occupational Centre. The title of the review was "*The Road To Wigan Pier Via Barnsley and South Yorkshire*". And here it is;

"*It has taken George Orwell (Down And Out In Paris And London, etc) 254 pages to get to Wigan Pier but whether he could have arrived at his delectable destination by turning Right rather than turning Left I don't know, but he has been an agreeable companion - not that I wholly agree with him but he helps us to see some things more clearly. Half way to this famous protruberance he halts and presumably refreshed gives a sort of "story of my life".*

"*It is particularly the first journey I want to tell you about because Orwell (he would not mind the Christian name, probably he would prefer it solus!) condescends to mention a town we all know something of - dear old Barnsley.*

"*On the way there are some delightful touches. A landlady "too ill to do anything but east stupendous meals". O glorious epigram.*

"*But it is when George as an unsophisticated layman takes us down a coal mine that he really excels and his words are thrilling without any overstatement. "The train bore me away through the monstrous scenery of chimneys, slagheaps, piled scrap iron, foul canals, paths of cindery mud criss-crossed by the prints of clogs.......Slag heaps and chimneys seem a more probable normal landscape than grass and trees......Our civilisation, pace Chesterton, is founded on coal.....The miner is a sort of grimy caryatid upon whose shoulders nearly everything that is not grimy is supported......". Orwell lived with a mining family for a short time and found out what we all know, what a splendid fellow he is, and how well he does work which any other person would consider as too arduous even to contemplate.*

"After quoting Ald. Joseph Jones' "Coal Scuttle" Orwell goes on about "the pit head baths are paid for wholly or partly by the miners themselves out of the Miners' Welfare Fund. Sometimes the colliery company subscribes, sometimes the Fund bears the whole cost.

"I refer the author to "The Coal Problems" (J.P. Dickie) pages 226, 227 and 229 for a more accurate account; "Chief among activities of the Welfare Fund Committee is the provision of pit head baths.....built out of monies provided by the levies on output and royalties. They are maintained (my italics) by the men's contributions, and by contributions from the owners which take various forms, either a cash or free heating and lighting service...The finance of the Welfare Fund is provided by a levy on the output, payable by the owners, and a charge on the royalties. When the fund was instituted it was financed entirely by a levy of 1d. per ton on the output. In 1926 the money available was supplemented by a levy of 5 per cent. on royalties and way leaves to be devoted to the provision of pit head baths. The 1d. per ton produced approximately a million per annum .and the royalties welfare levy approximately £200.000 per annum. In 1934 1d. was reduced to 1/2d. and made to apply retrospectively to the 1932 output levy (payable in 1933) while the duration was extended by 16 years to 1951.

"Housing in industrial areas comes in for some of Orwell's scourge and after mentioning Leeds, Sheffield and Wigan he proceeds to select three from this area for special vilification - one in Wortley Street and one in Peel Street, Barnsley, and one in Mapplewell. And then we come across this remarkable passage.

"One thing that always strikes me as mysterious is that so many of the northern towns see fit to build themselves immense and luxurious public buildings at the same time as they are in crying need of dwelling houses. The town of Barnsley, for instance, recently spent close on £150,000 on a new town hall, although admittedly needing at least 2,000 new working-class houses, not to mention public baths. (The public baths in Barnsley contain nineteen men's slipper baths--this in a town of 70,000 inhabitants, largely miners, not one of whom has a bath in his house!) For

£150,000 it could have built 350 Corporation houses and still had £10,000 to spend on a town hall. However, as I say, I do not pretend to understand the mysteries of local government. I merely record the fact that houses are desperately needed and are being built, on the whole, with paralytic slowness.

"George Orwell obviously did not see Barnsley's alleged Town Hall in the old days where the departments were scattered to the cardinal points of the town and where the assembly chamber was near to the police cells! For a County Borough of the size of Barnsley the town hall was a disgrace and the present building was necessary. Of course, I am not going to say that it is a perfect Town Hall, for there is waste room; some town halls include a public library, fire station, art school, and other departments which our town hall does not, but there is no point in going into all that. Is there anything in George's grumble that it is incompatible with good government to build a town hall while the need for houses exists? Unless we build houses night and day the need will always exist, and we should still be waiting for our town hall. And then that astounding statement about 70,000 largely miners with no baths {...} Mr Orwell, well well {...} The actual number in Barnsley engaged in mining and quarrying is 9,287 and there are about 3,200 Council houses each of which has a bath. Now I am not going to say that every miner lives in a Council house but a large number do and it is certainly well over the mark to say that not a miner in Barnsley has a bath in his house. And then we are not taking into account the houses - not Council houses - where there might be baths. There are 14,498 houses of a rateable value of £13 and under and we may assume that these are all inhabited by the working classes; deducting the council houses, surely out of the 11,298 we shall find a few with a bath in! It is a pity that George Orwell has not been better informed for it is statements like this that tend to subvert our faith in other parts of an otherwise excellent volume.

"Orwell deals quite rationally with complaints of people who have been transferred from appalling slum areas to the outskirts of the town; they feel the cold more and - a point we have often raised - the rents are higher and added to this is the cost of conveyance into the town. The author's solution is flats, but he is right about this type of people being prejudiced and in this apart Orwell is very fair indeed. He views slum clearance from all angles and he points out that a general clearance "from the point of view of the independent shopkeeper is a disaster.

Many a small shopkeeper is ruined utterly by some re-housing scheme which takes no notice of his existence......I sometimes think that the price of liberty is not so much eternal vigilance but eternal dirt...."

"I don't like Orwell's cheap gibes at social service work, and he may call me an oily bourgeois reactionary if he likes, but he has never been in the Barnsley Men's Centre obviously. If he has then his remarks are more unaccountable.

"But if he has not been to a centre he has been among the people and has plumbed their very depths as this; "When people live on the dole for years at a time they grow used to it, and drawing the dole, though it remains unpleasant, ceases to be shameful. Thus, the old, independent, workhouse-fearing tradition is undermined, just as the ancient fear of debt is undermined by the hire-purchase system. In the back streets of Wigan and Barnsley I saw every kind of privation, but I probably saw much less conscious misery than I should have seen ten years ago. The people have at any rate grasped that unemployment is a thing they cannot help. It is not only Alf Smith who is out of work now; Bert Jones is out of work as well, and both of them have been 'out' for years. It makes a great deal of difference when things are the same for everybody. So you have whole populations settling down, as it were, to a lifetime on the P.A.C. And what I think is admirable, perhaps even hopeful, is that they have managed to do it without going spiritually to pieces.

"There is much more I would like to say on this book which everyone should read, even if he has to wait a year to borrow it, but I feel like the reporter who was told to "do a column" only of a meeting. When he had got his column, he walked out of the meeting and left the other part entirely. This is what I am doing. My space is up and I only have room to say that George Orwell emphasises how courteously he was treated by the Yorkshire miner".

The Alderman Joseph Jones that Langstaff quoted to undermine Orwell's assertion about the financing of pit baths was the then mayor of Barnsley, also president of the Miners' Federation of Great Britain (MFGB), the forerunner of the National Union of Mineworkers (NUM), and also a former member of the National Executive Committee of the Labour Party, and was therefore as solid a source of evidence as the Chronicle's editor could have got to refute Orwell's claims.

As for the Town Hall however, things have gone full circle. There are now few departments still based there but it does now have a library, or the local studies centre, which now has copies of the notes, narrative and diaries that Orwell took from late January 1936 to late March 1936 in the very building that Orwell questioned the need for in them. He may now have been pleased with this irony but would have been less impressed, given his aversion to members of the English aristocracy who openly flirted with Hitler, that the Town Hall had been officially opened in 1933 by the then Prince Of Wales who by March 1936 and the time of Orwell's visit had become King Edward VIII. By March 1937, the publication of The Road To Wigan Pier's and the above review however he had abdicated to spend more time with his American wife and the German leader.

Other than pointing out its factual inaccuracies and criticising Orwell's comments about the Unemployment Occupational Centre and need for the new Town Hall, Langstaff was positive about the book. Given that an outsider, a published writer, was highlighting great social problems within the town it would have been cynically reactionary and counter-productive for the editor of the local newspaper to do anything else. The town had great problems and Langstaff would have been grateful for the publicity these problems got through Orwell.

However, it should be borne in mind that the editor of the main local newspaper would have wanted to keep as close with the council as possible. Orwell's criticism of the spending on the Town Hall would be a logical target for someone wanting to keep pally with the councillors but Langstaff was right to shoot Orwell down on this. Orwell would have been doing little other than repeat what he had heard among people without seeing the bigger picture. And he hadn't written anything similar about Wigan and Sheffield Town Halls presumably because they were Victorian and therefore not a financial bone of contention at the time he was there. Orwell's criticisms were little other than repeating locals' views without taking into account all sides of the argument.

There are however other possible inaccuracies in the book that Langstaff may have pointed out that had local relevance. For example, in chapter 2 he writes "It is not long since conditions in the mines were worse than they are now. There are still living a few very old women who in their

57

youth have worked underground...". This seems to have been based on his diary entry for 18th March where he writes *"There is a very old woman – a Lancashire woman – living near here who in her day has worked down the pit, dragging tubs of coal with a harness and chain. She is 83, so I suppose this would be in the seventies".*

If this were true then it would have been illegal. Women could work at the surface sorting coal or loading wagons but under the Mines and Collieries Act 1842 all females and all children under the age of ten had been banned from working underground in mines. In an act of humane benevolence however boys over the age of ten could then continue to work underground despite the legislation being a reaction to the Huskar Pit tragedy in Silkstone Common, Barnsley in 1838 when eleven girls aged from eight to sixteen and fifteen boys aged between nine and twelve were drowned underground as a result of a thunderstorm. Blessed are the lawmakers.

Tragedies like these no longer happen not just because working minimum age limits have increased but also because there are no deep coal mines left in the UK. In Barnsley the four pits that Orwell visited have all been closed for at least twenty-five years; Wentworth Silkstone closed in 1978, North Gawber in 1986, Barnsley Main in 1991 (it had originally closed in 1966 but was reopened in 1985 due to nearby Barrow colliery having to close because of geological problems) and Grimethorpe in 1992. The most visible evidence today of their existence is the remaining pithead headstock structure of Barnsley Main which is now grade II listed. This might come across as a sanitised apology for the end of the mining industry in Britain but welcome attempts have been made to preserve some of the mining heritage. This may seem strange given that mines were uglier than factories. They didn't have chimneys belching out smoke but coal dust permeated the air all round. That of course is no longer the case. And then there were the slagheaps around them. As Orwell wrote in chapter 7 of Barnsley; *"Often the slag-heaps are on fire, and at night you can see the red rivulets of fire winding this way and that, and also the slow-moving blue flames of sulphur, which always seem on the point of expiring and always spring out again".* You don't get that in an industrial heritage centre.

On the day he visited Barnsley Main, March 22nd, Orwell also walked with Ellis Firth and another unnamed local man along the canal by a nearby glass works. This would almost certainly have been Beatson Clark which was then situated right next door to both the Dearne and Dove Canal and Barnsley Main and which had recently been built on the site of the former Hope Glass Works which had been an off shoot of the nearby Rylands Glass Works and had closed a few years earlier (part of Barnsley Main had earlier been called Rylands Main Colliery). There were however other glass works besides Beatson Clark and Rylands on canals nearby including Woods at Hoyle Mill and Redfearns at Old Mill.

Hope alone had already employed over 1,000 men and boys fifty years before Orwell's visit. Woods was right on the Dearne and Dove Canal about half a mile south west from the pit back towards the town centre. Redfearns was next to Barnsley Canal about half a mile north west and past the confluence of the Dearne and Dove Canal and the Barnsley Canal by the river Dearne at Barnsley Junction. Both a miner and glass-maker still feature predominantly on the town's coat of arms so Orwell got the right local industries to visit.

The Barnsley Canal was built a hundred and forty years earlier to transport coal north to Wakefield and beyond. It closed within twenty years of Orwell's visit and the five-arched aqueduct at Hoyle Mill immediately north of the confluence of the two canals which carried barges over the river Dearne was demolished. Of all the local industrial landmarks this was an engineering feat that deserved to be preserved, but was instead torn down as it had been deemed unsafe for decades, being subject to subsidence caused by the pits whose coal it ferried, and was too expensive to maintain. The aqueduct was later replaced by a footbridge over the Dearne using the lower parts of the aqueduct's original supports.

The Dearne and Dove Canal, built just after the Barnsley Canal and also to transport coal, ran east to Swinton. One of its two branches, the Elsecar branch, served Cortonwood Colliery where the 1984 miners' strike began. Like the Barnsley Canal, the Dearne and Dove Canal closed in the post-war years. Both had been built in the pre-railway age and had suffered from a long-term decline in use. Much of both has been filled in and built over but parts of both remain. Sadly this doesn't include the part of the Dearne and Dove Canal that Orwell walked along by Barnsley Main pit and glassworks at Hoyle Mill although the route of the canal can still be traced there. Almost the entire Elsecar branch remains through to Brampton however although it's no longer navigable. It does though pass the remains of Hemingfield pit and some old miners cottages and even has a steam train running alongside it from Elsecar Heritage Centre.

As for the housing that Orwell visited, by the time of the The Road To Wigan Pier's publication, Barnsley council had started to build the large council estates away from the town centre to rehouse those moved out of the slums of Barebones and other back to back houses. By 1939 Wortley Street had been emptied of all its residents and Blucher Street of most of its. Peel Street however was still almost fully occupied. At the same time Kendray, Worsborough Common (which was built on the allotments of California Gardens that Orwell mentions in his notes) and Lundwood, all Barnsley's answer to Parson Cross, Wybourn, Manor and others in Sheffield, were largely in place. The rest of Barnsley have been reading the related court reports in the Barnsley Chronicle ever since. New Lodge and Athersley followed after the war. The Chronicle had to invest in a larger printing plant.

Town centre streets that had had slums demolished were no longer considered suitable for housing. Blucher Street and Wortley Street lost half their respective lengths thank to businesses and a relief road. Wortley Street is as nondescript today as Thomas Street in Sheffield is although it did get national publicity in 2017 when a couple were filmed having sex in broad daylight at 6 o'clock in the morning next to a church, not a good example of cleanliness being next to Godliness. Still at least it's not a slum any more. Albert Street East is now a shopping street alone, part of a concrete mess that is half the town centre, rebuilt in brutalist concrete style in the 1960s and 1970s and now being rebuilt again. Anything that Sheffield can do.

With his near two months of research complete Orwell returned to his sister and brother-in-law in Leeds on March 26th. His two weeks in Barnsley had gone unnoticed outside the circle of miners and the few others he met in town. The Barnsley Chronicle at the time makes no mention of him. Two days after he left, the headlines instead included a Holmfirth farmer being prosecuted for allowing his sheep to freeze to death, and of the first talkie film of religious songs to hit a Wombwell congregational church being a big hit among the local children. Still, only another 20 years till rock 'n' roll hits town, kids.

60

From Leeds he travelled back to London four days later. Within days he moved to a small cottage in Wallington in Hertfordshire, a Home Counties village as far from the industrial environment of Wigan, Sheffield and Barnsley as he could have chosen. Other than his diary and the notes and narrative that he took back with him the closest he may have got to the industrial north during the rest of 1936 was his first wife Eileen, a native of County Durham, whom he married two months later. The middle-class writer may have become so estranged from the factories and mines of the north that he wasn't even aware that Barnsley had avoided relegation by a point. Still, he wrote The Road To Wigan Pier over the rest of the year, observing from afar as Spain descended into civil war, handing the typescript to his agent Leonard Moore in December for The Left Book Club to publish three months later. At that point Orwell was looking south rather than north. The Road To Wigan Pier was behind him and Homage To Catalonia ahead.

Shortly afterwards Orwell went to war in Spain wearing a blue suit, emphasising that his two months among the hoi polloi hadn't given him any rough edges. His stay there would produce Homage To Catalonia, his third and last book of non-fiction and his sixth book in all. On the way he stopped off to see Henry Miller in Paris. If the two compared their respective recent works of Tropic of Cancer and The Road To Wigan Pier then Miller must rightly have been appalled by Orwell's tales of the debauched goings on among the beer and sandwiches of the South Yorkshire Branch of the Working Men's Club & Institute Union on Wellington Street compared to pre-war Paris. The Latin Quarter has been cleaned up a bit since but Wellington Street hasn't changed much, especially near Wortley Street.

Being in Spain prevented Orwell from proof-reading The Road To Wigan Pier before publication although he asked for just one minor change in the passage about his train journey over the Pennines. It was subsequently published in March 1937 while he was still in Spain. Orwell sent Henry Miller a complimentary copy but no miner in Yorkshire and Lancashire benefitted from such largesse.

Agnes Pit Yard by Pond Street 1937.

Orwell's lodgings on Agnes Terrace were roughly twenty yards to the left of the disused pit's entrance, now replaced by a lower concrete cap. At the back is part of Fleming Street which was razed along with the rest of Barebones in the 1960s. The path in the middle still links the bottom of Pond Street to the top.

Agnes Road and Wood Street 1937.

Back to back houses on Agnes Road (left) and Wood Street (right), all now demolished. Through the guincll on the right was the junction of these two streets, Princess Street and New Street. Orwell's lodgings on Agnes Terrace were about a hundred yards away.

Albert Street 1937.

Albert Street in the town centre looking north. Albert Street East where Ellis Firth lived and was visited by Orwell was off to the right. The clock tower of Barnsley Town Hall whose cost Orwell argued should have been spent on housing looms above in the background, the only building still surviving.

Blucher Street 1937.

Blucher Street where Orwell visited. At the end is the back of a house on Blucher Street with court houses on either side, looking west from near Wellington Street.

Wortley Street 1937.

Wortley Street where Orwell visited and mentioned in chapter IV of The Road To Wigan Pier, looking east towards Wellington Street.

Providence Street 1937

Providence Street where Orwell visited, next door to Pond Street, a hundred yards or so from where Orwell stayed.

The Canal, Pit and Glass Works

The Dearne and Dove Canal and Beatson Clark Glass Works at Hoyle Mill by Barnsley Main pit where Orwell and Ellis Firth walked. The canal wound from here at Stairfoot towards Beatson Clark Glass Works and from there to Barnsley Main pit next door and on to the junction with Barnsley Canal at Old Mill. A muckstack from Barnsley Main can be seen just above the buildings on the left. It doesn't seem to be on fire but give it a few minutes.

Epilogue

Our civilization, pace Orwell, is no longer founded on coal. Coal, like the Wigan Pier that Orwell went in search of but couldn't find as it had already been destroyed, is now little more than just part of British history. The Britain of 1936 that Orwell wrote about in The Road To Wigan Pier, some of which dated back to before the Industrial Revolution, began to be dismantled forty years or so after he returned south. Even before then it was under pressure. Nearly another forty years on, the Britain where trades union leaders are public figures is only a memory. The solar panel industry has no equivalent of Arthur Scargill. In 1936 the working class had the industrial muscle but not the material rewards. Today the opposite is true except in areas where even the poverty of today would be considered luxurious relative to that of 1936. If some areas hardly changed between Engels' work of 1844 and Orwell's of 1936 there is little left of either of them today outside of an industrial heritage centre. Admittedly new slums have been built since but conditions have improved greatly in general.

The industry of Barnsley and Sheffield was determined by geography - the coal seams and flowing water. The seams and rivers are still there but following privatisation of both the steel and coal industries they have shrunk massively, one to the point of extinction. In the fifty years to 2018 coal has declined from its peak of being the main source of energy produced in Britain to one which on some particular days isn't used to provide any electricity at all. Deep coal mining in Britain has disappeared completely. As for steel, in 1970 national output was four times higher than it had been when Orwell visited Sheffield. Half of Sheffield's workforce was employed in manufacturing. Today it is a quarter of that figure. Nationally over 320,000 people worked in the steel industry in 1970 but this figure has fallen by 90% in the fifty years since. Production has fallen by a similar ratio too.

With Britain's industrial decline the importance of education in the economy has grown massively. In chapter VII of The Road to Wigan Pier, Orwell compared how his middle class peers viewed education compared to how the working class viewed it. "*And again, take the working-class attitude towards 'education'. How different it is from ours, and how immensely sounder! Working people often have a vague reverence for learning in others, but where 'education' touches their own lives they see through it and reject it by a healthy instinct. I know now that there is not one working-class boy in a thousand who does not pine for the day when he will leave school. He wants to be doing real work, not wasting his time on ridiculous rubbish like history and geography".* Despite coal and steel being industries that were based on geography and which largely have become history, that same attitude towards education lives on. It may have been appropriate in 1936 but today when finding a job locally in Barnsley is no longer as easy as just knocking on the door of the nearest factory or pit, it is a passport only to low pay and no skills, or no pay at all.

Orwell recognised education as being one of the important class differences of the time. He arrived in northern England as a middle-class author and journalist and left as one. What he witnessed shaped his political views but not his instincts. He remained someone purely of the bourgeois literary world. In part one of The Road To Wigan Pier he wrote of them, the working class. In part two he also wrote of them, the working class as well as us, the literary middle-class. He named us, the writers. He didn't name them, the miners. Remember that the only person he named in the book who had gone down a mine was D H Lawrence. Down And Out In Paris And London didn't make him homeless and The Road To Wigan Pier didn't make him a miner, or working class. Jack Hilton, on whose advice Orwell ended up in Wigan and from there Barnsley and who therefore led Orwell to shape the book into one largely about miners and mining, described the book as *"piffle"* and a waste of money and energy on the basis that Orwell couldn't overcome the class differences between himself and the people he wrote about in the book, particularly the miners.

Orwell's remarks on education can be read as being condescending and patronising. It was good enough for him but fine if the working class didn't want it in their world. They had their own worries after all. In his 1940 essay Inside The Whale, reviewing Henry Miller's Tropic Of Cancer and the similarities reviewers had drawn between it and James Joyce's Ulysses, Orwell wrote *"What Miller has in common with Joyce is a willingness to mention the inane, squalid facts of everyday life".* Orwell may have been showing he was still interested in the inane, squalid facts of everyday life but it was the inane, squalid facts of everyday life as described in other writers' fiction that concerned him most, showing he was instinctively still the same journalist, writer and literary man he had been when he left London in January 1936 rather than a convert to the lifestyle he had seen in the north. Squalid life was seen primarily as a subject matter for the literary middle class to write about. So he sent Miller a gift in the form of a copy of his book but he didn't send the miners one. You suspect a sense of detachment and snobbery.

The same sense of detachment and an inverted snobbery can be found on the other side however. Monty Python's Working Class Playwright attitude lives on among many people who are either not suited to education or are hostile to it on principle, despite there being no more mining jobs. A lot of young people in Barnsley, though relatively few compared to in more affluent areas, do go off to university but there is little work to come back to with a degree. Barnsley Council has tried to attract big investment to the town but has been unable to bring in well-paid, skilled jobs. A Barnsley Council report in 2016 summarised as follows; "*Barnsley is relatively deprived in Education, Skills & Training, Employment, Health & Disability and Income ..... compared to the other local authorities in England*".

Sheffield has done much better. University graduates have a relatively high stay-on rate for work although in some spheres it can't offer the prospects that similar cities like Manchester, Leeds and Bristol can. Yet compared to Barnsley which loses educational attainment, Sheffield attracts the academically gifted to its two universities and keeps them. And Sheffield still makes some steel whereas the industry Barnsley is most famous for has completely gone. That isn't Barnsley's fault but the anti-education bias of a lot of working class people there lives on, one legacy of 1936 that really should have been lost along with the mines.

Health was an issue Orwell highlighted in the 1936 book and is mentioned still today in the above 2016 Barnsley report. Orwell died in hospital of tuberculosis in 1950. He was forty-six, twenty years younger than the average male life expectancy of the time. TB had been a disease he had witnessed often in the homes he visited in Lancashire and Yorkshire. He had had chest problems from infancy and his lifestyle choices in following his ambition to be a writer exacerbated his ill-health. Witness the mystery about how long he spent ill at the Deiners in

Liverpool after a trip down a Lancashire mine. The environment of Wigan, Sheffield and Barnsley in 1936 could not have helped him and ironically he died much younger even than many who suffered from working and living in these same environments for most or all of their lives.

Because of the decline of the industries that he came north to see and of legislation like the clean air acts and other environmental improvements, the environment is much cleaner now. The vista of factory chimneys and their smoke have gone and the rivers have been cleaned although new sources of pollution have replaced the factory smoke. Sheffield steel output is a fraction of what it was. The mines and their burning slagheaps have gone too as a result of a policy first implemented on bright cold day in March 1984.